Building a Windows IT
Infrastructure in the Cloud

David K. Rensin

Beijing · Cambridge · Farnham · Köln · Sebastopol · Tokyo

Building a Windows IT Infrastructure in the Cloud
by David K. Rensin

Published by O'Reilly Media, Inc., 1005 Gravenstein Highway North, Sebastopol, CA 95472.

O'Reilly books may be purchased for educational, business, or sales promotional use. Online editions are also available for most titles (*http://my.safaribooksonline.com*). For more information, contact our corporate/institutional sales department: 800-998-9938 or *corporate@oreilly.com*.

Editors: Andy Oram and Mike Hendrickson	**Cover Designer:** Karen Montgomery
Production Editor: Kara Ebrahim	**Interior Designer:** David Futato
Copyeditor: Rebecca Freed	**Illustrators:** Robert Romano and Rebecca Demarest
Proofreader: Kara Ebrahim	

Revision History for the First Edition:
   2012-09-24   First release
See *http://oreilly.com/catalog/errata.csp?isbn=9781449333584* for release details.

ISBN: 978-1-449-33358-4

[LSI]

1348503410

Table of Contents

Preface

Everybody's talking about cloud services today. It's one of the hot new buzzwords, but most of the conversation is about how to develop custom applications in the cloud. While that is a really important topic, it ignores another very useful attribute of a distributed cloud: as a *great* place to build and host an IT infrastructure.

The dearth of discussion about this overlooked facet of cloud computing is the reason I wrote this book. I was especially interested in discussing the topic in the context of the Amazon Web Services (AWS) cloud offering because it is my opinion that Amazon's service represents one of the most flexible and cost-effective of the major cloud vendors. I especially feel strongly that the AWS cloud is particularly well suited to hosting a custom IT infrastructure.

Apparently the good people at O'Reilly agreed!

Intended Audience

Are you an IT administrator (by choice or force)? Have you ever wondered what it might be like to run your entire corporate IT infrastructure in a cloud that you controlled completely?

If so, then this book is for you!

In this book I will walk you through how to set up a complete IT infrastructure in the AWS cloud. You don't need to have a lot of IT experience to follow along—just a willingness to try new things and experiment a bit.

Organization of This Book

The AWS cloud offering is one of the most comprehensive ever created. It also has the advantage of being owned and operated by a company that knows a thing or two about always-on availability! Those reasons alone make it a great place for a new IT infrastructure and a very interesting topic for a book.

This book is divided into eight chapters, each one guiding you through the process of adding a critical service to your new IT cloud.

Chapter 1, *To the Cloud!*, is a basic introduction to the AWS cloud and lays the basic foundation for your new network. In it you will configure a VPN in order to securely access your growing family of resources.e

Chapter 2, *Directories, Controllers, and Authorities—Oh My!*, will show you how to transform your network into a real enterprise infrastructure by creating a Windows domain.

Chapter 3, *Let There Be Email!*, will guide you through the process of setting up enterprise email using Microsoft Exchange. You will also learn the basics of special DNS records called *Mail Exchanger* (MX) records and how to create your own managed DNS in the AWS cloud.

Chapter 4, *Doing Things the Easy Way*, will bring you up close and personal with some of the very powerful command-line tools that Amazon gives you. In particular you will learn how to take your custom-made virtual machine and import it directly into your virtual network.

Chapter 5, *Do You Have Some Time to Chat?*, will cover the fastest growing form of enterprise communication: chat. Yes, you read that right. Chat/instant messaging is starting to take over in the enterprise, and in this chapter you will learn how to set up your own services to support it.

Chapter 6, *The Voice of a New Generation*, will guide you through installing and configuring your very own voice-over-IP (VoIP) system so you can make and receive Internet-based telephone calls in your growing enterprise.

Chapter 7, *Keeping Your Network Fit, Trim, and Healthy*, will introduce you to the tools you will use to keep your new network healthy and safe. They include backup and restore, intrusion detection, and fault alerting.

Chapter 8, *For Those About to Grok, We Salute You*, the final chapter, will take you under the hood of some of the more complicated topics covered in the previous chapters. This chapter is optional reading and is intended for people who like to take things apart just to see how they work.

 A quick word about the chapter titles. Many of the titles and section headings of the chapters are bad puns. They cover the waterfront from the Old Testament to famous science fiction, heavy metal hits, and something my great-grandmother used to say in Yiddish. None of them are particularly obscure (even the one from my great-grandmother) but if you should find yourself struggling to get the reference, feel free to drop me a line at *dave@rensin.com*.

Conventions Used in This Book

The following typographical conventions are used in this book:

Italic
> Indicates new terms, URLs, email addresses, filenames, and file extensions.

`Constant width`
> Used for program listings, as well as within paragraphs to refer to program elements such as variable or function names, databases, data types, environment variables, statements, and keywords.

`Constant width bold`
> Shows commands or other text that should be typed literally by the user.

`Constant width italic`
> Shows text that should be replaced with user-supplied values or by values determined by context.

 This icon signifies a tip, suggestion, or general note.

 This icon indicates a warning or caution.

Using Code Examples

This book is here to help you get your job done. In general, you may use the code in this book in your programs and documentation. You do not need to contact us for permission unless you're reproducing a significant portion of the code. For example, writing a program that uses several chunks of code from this book does not require permission. Selling or distributing a CD-ROM of examples from O'Reilly books does require permission. Answering a question by citing this book and quoting example code does not require permission. Incorporating a significant amount of example code from this book into your product's documentation does require permission.

We appreciate, but do not require, attribution. An attribution usually includes the title, author, publisher, and ISBN. For example: "*Building a Windows IT Infrastructure in the Cloud* by David K. Rensin (O'Reilly). Copyright 2012 David K. Rensin, 978-1-449-33358-4."

If you feel your use of code examples falls outside fair use or the permission given above, feel free to contact us at *permissions@oreilly.com*.

Acknowledgments

I wrote my last book in 1997. Back then I was sure that I was done writing books. When I put away my word processor for what I thought would be the last time, I had failed to meet only one of my objectives in becoming an author—to write a book for O'Reilly Media.

When I was in college and really starting to cut my teeth as a programmer, the O'Reilly catalog of books was incomprehensibly valuable to me in my learning. Titles like *sed & awk*, *lex and yacc*, *Programming Perl*, *High Performance Computing*, and others taught me much of what I still hold dear as a programmer.

They were books written by geeks for geeks and I read as many as I could get my hands on.

Back then I would never have dreamed that one day I would get the chance to contribute to that library, and I will forever be grateful to Tim O'Reilly for creating this one special place where all these wonderful books could get published.

I would also like to thank Mike Hendrickson, who read my proposal, liked it, and got it green-lighted by the editorial board. He's the one who let me jump from O'Reilly fan to O'Reilly author, and for that he will forever have my thanks.

Andy Oram has been the most patient editor I've ever worked with. He's gone to bat for me on issues large and small, has provided unvarnished and exceptionally helpful commentary on the content, and has been an all-around good guy to work with. Thank you, Andy!

My wife Lia has long suspected my sanity. When I told her I wanted to write another book, I am certain her suspicions were immediately confirmed. The look on her face struck me as how one might look after having been slapped suddenly with a dead fish.

Her entirely reasonable reservations aside, she has never once complained about all the time writing has taken from her and our three children, or all the house chores that have gone ignored while I've been holed up in my office beavering away.

In the 21 years we've been together she's put up with a lot from me. Crazy business ideas. Crazy book ideas. Crazy parenting ideas. You name it and she's had to deal with it.

My darling, it is to you that I am most grateful. Not for putting up with all my craziness, but for seeing something in me worth putting up with. I love you in a way that words could never reflect and give thanks every day to the Big Editor in the Sky that I have you in my life.

Finally, I strongly encourage you, the reader, to send me comments, good and bad. I have endeavored to create something you will enjoy and profit from, but I have no doubt made errors in both fact and style.

You can reach me at *dave@rensin.com* and I hope you will not be bashful in doing so.

Safari® Books Online

 Safari Books Online (*www.safaribooksonline.com*) is an on-demand digital library that delivers expert content in both book and video form from the world's leading authors in technology and business.

Technology professionals, software developers, web designers, and business and creative professionals use Safari Books Online as their primary resource for research, problem solving, learning, and certification training.

Safari Books Online offers a range of product mixes and pricing programs for organizations, government agencies, and individuals. Subscribers have access to thousands of books, training videos, and prepublication manuscripts in one fully searchable database from publishers like O'Reilly Media, Prentice Hall Professional, Addison-Wesley Professional, Microsoft Press, Sams, Que, Peachpit Press, Focal Press, Cisco Press, John Wiley & Sons, Syngress, Morgan Kaufmann, IBM Redbooks, Packt, Adobe Press, FT Press, Apress, Manning, New Riders, McGraw-Hill, Jones & Bartlett, Course Technology, and dozens more. For more information about Safari Books Online, please visit us online.

How to Contact Us

Please address comments and questions concerning this book to the publisher:

> O'Reilly Media, Inc.
> 1005 Gravenstein Highway North
> Sebastopol, CA 95472
> 800-998-9938 (in the United States or Canada)
> 707-829-0515 (international or local)
> 707-829-0104 (fax)

We have a web page for this book, where we list errata, examples, and any additional information. You can access this page at *http://oreil.ly/windows-it*.

To comment or ask technical questions about this book, send emails to *bookquestions@oreilly.com*.

For more information about our books, courses, conferences, and news, see our website at *http://www.oreilly.com*.

Find us on Facebook: *http://facebook.com/oreilly*

Follow us on Twitter: *http://twitter.com/oreillymedia*

Watch us on YouTube: *http://www.youtube.com/oreillymedia*

## CHAPTER 1

To the Cloud!

Every few years the technology punditry anoints a new buzzword to rule them all. In the last ten years we've seen *mobile, social, Web 2.0, location-based services,* and others lay claim to the mantle. Some have stood the test of time. Most haven't. One idea, however, has managed to weather the vicissitudes of the buzzword sea—*cloud computing.*

At its core, cloud computing simply means running one's computing processes in someone else's physical infrastructure. Over the last decade this concept has seen many incarnations. In the early 2000s Larry Ellison (the CEO of Oracle) proclaimed that all user data would live in the cloud and that our computers would be little more than dumb terminals to get to the Web. He called this *network computing.* Of course, Larry's vision never completely materialized, but aspects of it are very much present in our lives today.

Take email, for example. A growing number of users are getting email from virtual providers like Gmail and Hotmail. These are cloud services (sometimes referred to as *Application Service Providers,* or ASPs). Another great example of the migration to the cloud is Google Calendar and Google Docs. Both services store our data in the cloud for consumption from whatever PC we happen to be in front of.

Services like DropBox let us store and share files in the cloud, while Microsoft's Office for the Web lets us move our entire Word, Excel, PowerPoint, and Outlook experience to the cloud.

YouTube, Vimeo, Hulu, and Netflix allow us to get our video entertainment from the cloud, while Pandora, Zune, Rhapsody, Spotify, and others do the same for music. Apple's iCloud, Google's Play, and Amazon Music even let us store our personal music libraries in the cloud for streaming anywhere and anytime.

These are all wonderful services that make life a lot easier for millions of people—your author included.

There are also services wherein a company's entire IT infrastructure is configured and run in the cloud. These are great options for new companies that don't want to spend a lot of money on new hardware or a dedicated IT staff. Not surprisingly, however, these services tend to force organizations to select from a fairly rigid menu of options —rather than letting the organization tailor services specifically to their needs. This creates an unfortunate trade-off between ease of use and administration on the one hand and breadth of reconfigurability on the other.

In a perfect world, however, there would be a place in the cloud where someone like you (and me, for that matter) could go to install and completely configure your own IT setup and run it for a few hundred dollars a month.

There is, and I'm going to show you exactly how to do it!

Who I Think You Are and Why I Think You Care

This book is for you do-it-yourself types who think standing up your own IT infrastructure in the cloud would be cool and don't want to be artificially limited by the constraints of an all-in-one provider.

Installing software doesn't scare you.

Editing the Windows registry doesn't make you break out in hives.

You don't need to be an IT expert by any stretch to get the most from this book, but before we go any further I should call out some of the things I expect you'll at least have heard of before reading on.

DHCP (Dynamic Host Control Protocol)
> It's the thing that assigns network settings to your computer so you don't have to do it by hand.

DNS (Domain Name Services)
> It's how a human-friendly name like *www.amazon.com* is translated into a machine-friendly IP address.

Windows domain
> A group of related computing resources on your network.

Active directory
> Keeps tracks of all your users and computing assets in a Windows domain.

If this is the first time you've ever heard of one or more of these terms, then this book may be a smidgen advanced for you. If, on the other hand, each of these terms at least rings a bell, then you're good to go.

So limber up those typing and clicking fingers because we're about to build us a gen-u-ine corporate IT infrastructure in the cloud. We're going to do it right, and best of all, we're going to do it inexpensively.

Before we jump in, though, I'd like to take a moment to introduce you to the most powerful set of cloud services on the Net today: Amazon Web Services.

Introducing Amazon Web Services

I don't think it will come as any surprise to you that Amazon runs some of the largest and most sophisticated data centers and data clouds ever constructed. You may even know that Amazon provides scalable development infrastructures for people wanting to write high-transaction and highly fault-tolerant software systems. What you may not know is that Amazon also provides a complete set of IT tools for organizations that want to create dedicated virtual clouds while retaining complete configuration control over their environments. These services—both developer and IT—are collectively known as *Amazon Web Services*.

As of the time of this writing (Amazon is adding new services all the time) the following is a list of the services Amazon offers to people.

CloudFormation
Allows a user to define a template of machine and service configurations that can then be instantiated with a single click. This template can include other Amazon services like EC2, VPC, Elastic Beanstalk, and others. Think of this service as a means of replicating a complicated IT and application infrastructure in just a few clicks.

CloudFront
A content delivery platform that scales to meet large simultaneous demands—great for distributing widely consumed digital goods like music and video.

CloudWatch
Enables you to collect, view, and analyze metrics related to your cloud resources. It's very helpful as your virtual infrastructure grows more complicated.

DynamoDB
If you are at all familiar with databases, you have probably been using relational database systems like Oracle or SQL Server. Over the last several years a new class of database system has emerged, generally referred to as *NoSQL* systems owing to the fact that they do not use SQL as their principal query language. These systems are popular for very large data sets that have to scale horizontally automatically. The downside is that they are often limited in the kinds of queries that can be performed against the data they hold. The Amazon DynamoDB service provides an infinitely scalable NoSQL system to programmers.

Elastic Compute Cloud (EC2)
Amazon EC2 is a service you'll be making heavy use of in this book. It's the service that lets you stand up and manage multiple virtual servers and will form the backbone of the virtual network we will build.

ElastiCache
Sometimes a developer needs to store a large amount of data in memory but does not need to commit it permanently to a database system. This typically happens in high-transaction-volume applications. For this use there is Amazon's

ElastiCache service, which provides highly scalable in-memory storage for large but transient data sets.

Elastic Beanstalk

For developers who don't want to worry about standing up the various Amazon service components they might need for their application, there is Elastic Beanstalk. Basically, Elastic Beanstalk is a programming framework that handles all the administration of your various needed services for you. You just write your application using the Beanstalk components, and it will worry about which services to provision on your behalf and how to scale them.

Elastic MapReduce

Storing large data sets in the cloud is one thing. Analyzing them for hidden meaning is something else entirely. This is where Amazon Elastic MapReduce (EMR) comes in. It is a service that helps you slice and dice the various data sets you have stored in any of the Amazon data storage services. If you're going to need to do serious analysis on data that you will be continuously collecting, then this is the service for you!

Identity and Access Management (IAM)

Amazon IAM is the framework under which you manage users who will have access to components of your Amazon services. For example, suppose you want to give one user access to a server instance you have set up using EC2 and another user administrative access to some data you have stored in DynamoDB. This is the service with which you would define those permissions. This book won't make use of this service, as you'll handle access control via the normal domain-credentialing system of Windows Server.

Relational Database Service (RDS)

If you're not quite ready to jump on board the NoSQL bandwagon, then the Amazon RDS should make you feel right at home. It's a scalable managed database system using the SQL query language and tools with which any experienced database administrator should be familiar.

Route 53

This is Amazon's scalable DNS system. Rather than setting up DNS names for machines using the tools of your domain provider (the people with whom you registered your domain name), you'll maintain your DNS zones and subzones using Route 53.

Simple Email Service (SES)

If you think you will need to send bulk email messages, then this is the service for you. Rather than setting up your own outbound email servers, you can use this service to do all the heavy lifting.

Simple Notification Service (SNS)

SNS allows developers and administrators to send out email and SMS alerts. Since you're going to configure your own email gateway, you're not going to make much use of this. But if you're a developer considering using the Amazon cloud for your application, this is a great way to integrate notifications without having to worry about the particulars of various SMS and email platforms and gateways.

Simple Queue Service (SQS)

Sometime developers will want different applications (or application components) to pass information among themselves. One of the best ways to do this is with a message queuing system. This service isn't covered in this book, but if you are planning on writing a distributed application, then you will definitely want to check this out.

Simple Storage Service (S3)

Think of this as your very own DropBox or other Internet file storage system. This is a great way to securely store vital information in a way that conforms to your enterprise security policies. It's also a really handy place to keep periodic backups of your production systems. You'll be making heavy use of this service later in the book, for backup and restore scenarios in the cloud.

Simple Workflow Service (SWF)

Highly distributed systems (like SETI) divide large problems into smaller work units called *tasks*. SWF is a service that lets application components set up, schedule, and manage the tasks specific to your large distributed process.

Storage Gateway

The Amazon Storage Gateway service is a really handy tool that lets you set up storage managed by Amazon that connects via the Internet to an appliance or PC sitting in your physical infrastructure. It's a fabulous way to do backups, disaster recovery, and archiving.

Virtual Private Cloud (VPC)

This service will be the backbone of this book and of your virtual IT infrastructure. In a nutshell, it allows you to collect server instances running on the Amazon EC2 service into a single (or segmented) virtual network. This means you can have your virtual domain controller talking to your virtual email server as if they were attached to the same bit of Ethernet—even though they may be across town from one another. I'll be spending *a lot* of time on this topic as we move along.

The Plan of Attack

Now that the introductions are out of the way, let's talk about how you're going to use these services to build your new IT infrastructure.

For the purposes of this book, I am going to walk you through installing the following list of IT services in your own network. There are countless others you can add, of course, but these are the ones I think are key to any true enterprise infrastructure.

- A Primary Domain Controller (PDC)
- An email server

- A chat server
- A voice over IP (VoIP) PBX
- A secure VPN infrastructure
- An automatic backup and restore process

In short, you want a completely functional IT system for immediate use.

To achieve this you will use the following five Amazon services:

- VPC
- EC2
- CloudWatch
- Route 53
- S3

By the time you are done with this book you will have a fully functioning IT infra-structure that you can run for less than $300 per month.

The 13 or so other services described earlier are really for any software developers you might have in your organization. There are some really great O'Reilly books that cater to people wanting to write scalable custom applications. This book, however, is not that. This is about the nuts and bolts of configuring an IT system that you can begin using immediately.

Before we go any further I'm going to assume that you have already signed up for a free Amazon Web Services account. If you haven't, please visit *http://console.aws.amazon.com* and create yourself a new account. If you already have a regular Amazon consumer account, this process will take no more than 30 seconds.

Setting Up the Domain and DNS

For the sake of this book I'm going to assume that you want to have a public-facing domain name (à la *MyCompany.com*). The first step in getting this is to pick a name not already in use and register it with a domain registrar.

A domain registrar is a company authorized by ICANN (Internet Corporation for Assigned Names and Numbers—the body that governs domain names for the Internet) to register and reserve domain names. Usually, each registrar is limited to specific top-level domains (TLDs) that are often restricted by country. For example, US-based registrars are usually limited to .com, .edu, .org, .gov, .us, .info, .co, and .me domains. A registrar in the UK might be limited to .co.uk or other UK-specific domains.

For the sake of our work here, I'm going to register the domain *DKRDomain.com*. Since *DKR* are my initials (David K. Rensin) I'm not likely to forget it!

You can use any registrar you want to reserve your domain. In my case, I used the cheapest one I could find—godaddy.com (*www.godaddy.com*). It was a 2-minute process and cost me $10 for the year.

The next thing I want to do is to have an AWS service named *Amazon Route 53* manage the DNS for my new domain. Route 53 is a complete DNS solution provided by Amazon that lets you control every aspect of the name resolution process for your domain.

By default, your registrar will want to manage all the DNSs for your domain.

That's no good.

Legitimate control freaks like me want to do it themselves. I need to tell the people I used to register my new domain to take a hike and let Route 53 do it for me. This way I have complete control over things.

To do likewise, first you need to go to the Route 53 page in the AWS online console. The URL for that is *https://console.aws.amazon.com/route53/home*. Since you already have a domain, you want to click the "Migrate an existing domain to Amazon Route 53" link. The steps to perform the migration are pretty straightforward.

1. Create a new hosted zone.
2. Go to the record sets.
3. Write down the values for the NS (name server) record set.
4. Go to the provider where you registered your domain and edit the zone file (or DNS server information) to match the values you just wrote down.

Figure 1-1. A sample hosted zone

Figure 1-2. The completed record sets

In my particular case, the correct screen on the *http://www.godaddy.com* site looks like this:

Figure 1-3. Editing the zone file on the GoDaddy site

You can confirm that your new DNS zone info is correct via a number of websites. Please keep in mind that it can take as long as 24 hours for the new information to make its way around the Internet, but in practice it usually takes only 5 to 10 minutes.

A simple and free site for DNS checking is *http://network-tools.com/nslook/*. All you have to do is fill in your new domain name and set the record type to NS (Name Server).

Now, whenever you want to add a new host to your domain (for example *www.dkrdomain.com*) all you have to do is go to the Route 53 page and add an *A Record* to your domain that maps your hostname (*www.dkrdomain.com*) to a specific IP address (173.172.171.170).

Setting Up Your Security Credentials

Before you can do anything interesting with either VPCs or EC2 instances, you must first set up at least one set of security credentials—known as a *key pair*. From the main Amazon management console, select the EC2 tab at the top. On the left-hand side of the screen, click the Key Pairs link near the bottom. Since there will almost certainly not be any key pairs already generated for you, select the ⬛ Create Key Pair button from the

```
NsLookup                                          Query the DNS for resource records

    domain   dkrdomain.com            query type   NS - Name server          ▼

    server   67 222 132 199           query class  IN - Internet      ▼

      port   53                       timeout (ms) 5000

        no recursion        advanced output        go

67.222.132.199 is a non-cached DNS Server

[67.222.132.199] returned a non-authoritative response in 234 ms:
Answer records

name            class  type  data                      time to live

dkrdomain.com   IN     NS    ns64.domaincontrol.com    3600s  (1h)

dkrdomain.com   IN     NS    ns63.domaincontrol.com    3600s  (1h)

dkrdomain.com   IN     NS    ns-781.awsdns-33.net      3600s  (1h)

dkrdomain.com   IN     NS    ns-53.awsdns-06.com       3600s  (1h)

dkrdomain.com   IN     NS    ns-2003.awsdns-58.co.uk   3600s  (1h)

dkrdomain.com   IN     NS    ns-1230.awsdns-25.org     3600s  (1h)

Authority records

[none]

Additional records

[none]

-- end --
```

Figure 1-4. NSLookup results for DKRDomain.com

top of the screen. Give your new key pair a name (I used DKR-EC2 since it was the key pair for my EC2 work—I strongly suggest that you follow a similarly consistent convention for yourself). When you click the Create button, the key pair file (it will end in the extension .pem) will automatically be downloaded to your computer.

 Save this key pair file someplace safe, where you know you can find it again. It will be *absolutely vital* to just about everything you do in the rest of this book!

Setting Up Your First Virtual Private Cloud

As I mentioned before, the virtual IT infrastructure we're going to set up will exist in its own private virtual network, or *VPC*. It follows, thusly, that the first thing you want to do is to create your new VPC. To do this, log in to the Amazon AWS Management Console (*https://console.aws.amazon.com*) and select the VPC tab. You will be greeted with a screen that looks like this:

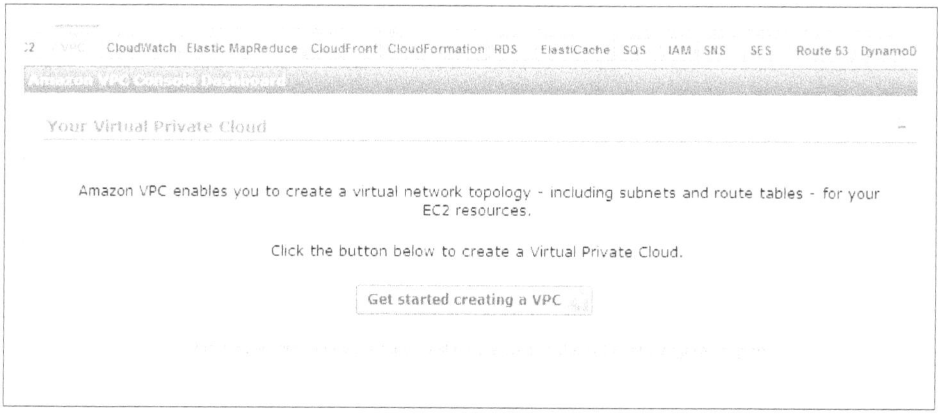

Figure 1-5. The AWS VPC starting screen

Click the "Get started creating a VPC" button.

Figure 1-6. Select a VPC type

AWS allows you to create some very complicated virtual infrastructures that include support for multiple subnets, hardware VPN connections to a data center, and mixed public/private subnets. For now, select the first option: VPC with a Single Public Subnet Only. This topology will do fine as long as you're appropriately security conscious.

On the next screen leave the defaults as they are, and click Create VPC. Once Amazon is done creating your new VPC, click the Close button. You VPC console page should now look like this:

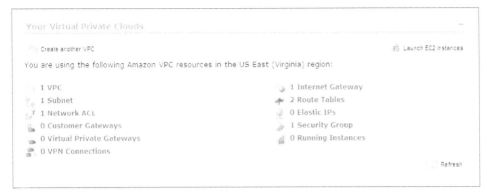

Figure 1-7. The updated VPC console page

Now that you have a new virtual network, take a look at just what Amazon has created for you.

1. There is, of course, one instance of a basic VPC shell.

2. Amazon created a default network access control list (ACL) for you. This is where you can modify firewall rules for specific virtual network interfaces. In truth, you will almost never touch these rules and should therefore leave them as is.

3. Since you want your new network to connect to the Internet, AWS has helpfully created a default Internet gateway.

4. You have two routing tables: one for traffic to and from the Internet and another for routing packets among machines in the network.

5. Finally, AWS created a default security group. Security groups are a great way to partition machines from one another and limit the sort of intermachine traffic you allow. The default group that has been set up says it will allow any traffic among machines in that group but deny any traffic for anyone else. This is a good first rule to have, so you should leave it be.

The last thing you want to do is to set up a single, public-facing IP address for your new VPC. While still in the VPC tab, select the Elastic IPs link on the left-hand side of the page. On the top of the page, click the ⚡ Allocate New Address button. The following screen should appear:

Figure 1-8. Allocate your new IP address for your VPC

Please note that this new public-facing IP address is not yet attached to any specific machine in your virtual infrastructure. You'll get to that a little further along.

Standing Up Your First Server Instance

So now that you have your virtual environment configured, it's time to set up your first server. You might think that—as is common in a Windows-based network—the domain controller would be the first machine you would want to configure, but that turns out to be not so. The first server you want to get running is actually the VPN server.

Why, you ask?

The answer is actually pretty simple. If you design security into your new infrastructure right from the beginning, you will be a lot less likely to be plugging holes later on. In this case, you want to limit all communications with the new environment and the outside world to a single secure channel. Eventually you'll open other services like Web and email, but while you're busy configuring things, the safest path to follow is one where everything is done via a VPN.

Choosing Your VPN Configuration

There are basically two types of VPN solutions in the world—IPsec and Secure Sockets Layer (SSL). As you might imagine, each solution has its pros and cons.

Most popular VPN solutions, like those from Cisco, are based on IPsec and are in very broad use. IT managers have a lot of experience with these kinds of VPNs, and most firewalls and routers support them. They do, however, have a couple of important downsides. First, they are almost always based on the User Datagram Protocol (UDP), versus TCP, and can have real problems getting through firewalls that use Network Address Translation (NAT). NATed infrastructures are extremely common in hotel WiFi configurations and can cause serious headaches when you're trying to dial back to your office.

The other serious drawback to IPsec VPNs is that there isn't any good free or open source server software for them. There are plenty of free clients, but if you want to set up a server in your infrastructure to actually enable the VPN connection, then you can expect to pay anywhere from a few hundred dollars to several thousand dollars for the privilege.

 Before you fire up your email to send me a nastygram about how Windows Server 2008 can, in fact, be configured as an IPsec VPN server, I would like to point out the following facts:

1. Both the Layer 2 Tunneling Protocol (L2TP) and Point-to-Point Tunneling Protocol (PPTP) network types that you could configure are generally regarded as being not safe.

2. The other option—Secure Socket Tunneling Protocol (SSTP)—is certainly safe enough, but almost no clients support it on a non-Windows platform. That means no Mac, Android, or iOS.

SSL VPNs are newer to the security market than their IPsec brethren. Almost no operating systems natively support them, which means you will always need to install a client on the device you want to use to make the connection. On the other hand, there are some really great free implementations you can use in your infrastructure. In addition, SSL VPNs can be configured to run via TCP (instead of UDP) and will *always* work in NATed network environments. This is precisely how you're going to set up your VPN.

All things being equal, I'm going to use an SSL VPN named *OpenVPN* to set up a secure channel in the example network. You can read more about OpenVPN at the OpenVPN main site (*http://www.OpenVPN.net/*).

Picking an AMI and Launching It Into Your VPC

One fantastic aspect of the Amazon Web Services is that many people have already done really interesting and difficult things using them. If, for example, we were going to set up a VPN server in our physically local space we would have to

1. Buy a PC.
2. Install an operating system.
3. Install and configure the VPN server software.

In the Amazon cloud, however, you can really shorten this process. For most common tasks—including setting up a VPN server—it is highly likely that someone has already done it and saved a snapshot of their running instance as an Amazon Machine Instance (AMI). That means if someone has already saved an OpenVPN AMI, for example, then you don't have to do anything more than create a new server instance in the cloud based on that AMI and tailor its configuration to your liking. That reduces a multihour process to less than 30 minutes.

Step 1 in the process is to find an appropriate AMI and launch it into your VPC. From the EC2 part of your management console, select Launch Instance.

In the window that pops up, select Quick Launch Wizard → More Amazon Machine Images, and name the new instance something useful like *Gateway*. Then select Continue.

Figure 1-9. Launching a new instance

On the next screen, type **DKR** in the search window, pick the DKR OpenVPN Server instance type, and click Continue. As you might have guessed from the AMI name, I've already built you a stock VPN server and made it available publicly.

Figure 1-10. Selecting and naming the new instance

The summary screen that appears shows the basic details of the instance you're about to launch. Notice that the item labeled Launch into a VPC is set to *No*. You want to change that.

1. Click the "Edit details" button and check the box on the next screen marked Launch into a VPC.

2. If you had more than one VPC to choose from, you could select it from the Subnet drop-down.

3. The type of instance currently configured for this AMI is a *t1.micro*. This is the smallest computing instance available in AWS. Unfortunately, you cannot launch a t1.micro instance into a VPC, so you need to select the next smallest unit— *m1.small*—from the Type drop-down list.

4. Select the Security Settings section and make sure that only the *default* security group is selected.

5. Click "Save details."

Now you can launch the new instance by clicking the Launch button.

It all goes well, you should be greeted with a success message like the following:

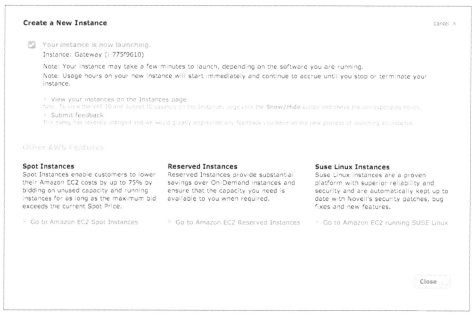

Figure 1-11. Success!

 New Windows instances can take upwards of 15 minutes to boot and be ready to use. Please wait until you see in the Instances section of the EC2 tab that your new instance is ready to go and that both of the status checks are green.

Connecting for the First Time

Before we can connect to your new server for the first time, you have to do two things:

1. Attach your external IP address to the server.
2. Enable use of the Remote Desktop Protocol (RDP).

First, establish a route from the Internet to your newly minted VPN server. In the AWS Management Console, select the VPC tab. On the left-hand side, click the Elastic IPs link. Now right-click the Elastic IP (EIP) you set up earlier and choose Associate. You should see the following:

Associate Address   Cancel ×

Select the instance or network interface to which you wish
to associate this IP address to.

Instance: ✓ **Select an instance**
                     i-9b0cc5fc – Gateway
or

Network Interface: Select a network interface ⌄

                              Cancel   Yes, Associate

Figure 1-12. Choose an instance to associate

Now select the instance you just created from the drop-down and click Yes, Associate.

The next thing you have to do is modify your default security rules to allow traffic on the standard RDP port: 3389.

Still on the VPC tab, click the link on the left-hand side labeled Security Groups. Now select the *default* group. Your browser should look like this:

Figure 1-13. Setting the default security group

Click the Inbound tab at the bottom of the screen and then click the Custom TCP rule drop-down. Next, scroll to the bottom and select RDP. Now click the Add Rule button and the Apply Rule Changes button. Your screen should look similar to this:

Figure 1-14. Our new security rules

What you've done is to allow RDP packets to flow into your newly created server.

 To access the new VPN server for the first time you will need an RDP client for your computer. If you're on a Windows machine, then you already have one built in (mstsc.exe). On the Mac I recommend downloading the Remote Desktop Connection client for Mac OS X from the Microsoft web page.

Next, you need to open a remote desktop to the new machine and perform some configuration. First, open your RDP client and enter in the server field the public IP address that you were given when you created your elastic IP for the VPC. Next, click the Connect button. You will be prompted for a username and password. Use the username **Administrator** and the password **passw0rd!**. Click the Connect button, and in a few moments you should have a remote desktop on the VPN instance.

 The very first thing you *must* do is change the password for the Administrator account. You can do this from the Control Panel applet as you would normally do on a Windows machine. I cannot stress this enough. Every person reading this book and using that AMI will have the same initial password, so be sure to change it straight away.

Now, let's chat for a few paragraphs about how the VPN server works.

Understanding and Configuring Your VPN Server

If you've ever used a VPN before, you're probably used to having to remember a username and password combination to authenticate. That's one way to set up a VPN. The other way to do it is to issue certificates for each user who will need to connect. The certificate acts as your password and keeps you from having to remember any extra information. The downside, of course, is that you *must* have your certificate on whichever machine you want to connect from.

Although the OpenVPN software can be configured to operate in either mode, I've configured the example's instance to use certificates instead of passwords.

Creating Your Own Client Certificate

To use this VPN you'll need to create your own client certificates for every user you want to allow to connect.

In any system that uses certificates, those certificates are stored in a place known as the *keystore*. OpenVPN is no different. Here are the steps to create your own client certificate so you can start using the VPN.

1. Still on the remote instance machine, open a Windows command prompt and type `cd "\Program Files (x86)\OpenVPN\easy-rsa"`.

2. Type `vars.bat`.

3. Type `build-key.bat client`. This starts a process that builds a client certificate. You don't have to use the name *client*. You can use `build-key.bat myCert` or some other name. Just make sure to remember what you used!

4. Answer the questions that are put to you.

> How you answer the questions is pretty much irrelevant except for when you get asked for the *common name*. That value *must* be unique among your certificates, or you won't be able to successfully store your certificate in the keystore.

5. Answer any yes or no questions **Yes**.

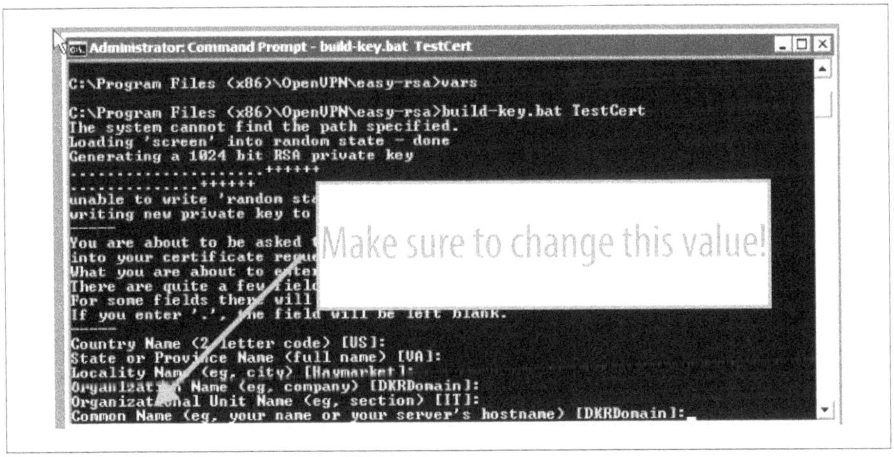

Figure 1-15. Pay close attention to this question

Congratulations! You now have a brand-spanking-new certificate named *client.crt*. This file is located in the **keys** subdirectory. In that directory, the three files you will need to make your client connection work are *ca.crt*, *client.crt*, and *client.key*. Keep in mind that you want the *.crt* and *.key* files that match the name you used when you ran `build-key.bat`.

Setting Up Your Client Machine and Connecting for the First Time

You already know that you will need copies of the three certificate files from above on your local computer. How you get them there is really a matter of personal preference.

- The easiest way is to go into the preferences section of your RDP client and tell it that you want to share drives. When you do this, the drives from your local machine will show up under My Computer on the VPN server. You can just copy the files directly.

- You can also use a file-sharing service like DropBox (*http://www.DropBox.com*) to transfer the files.

- If you have a Web email account like Gmail, then you can just email the files to yourself from the VPN box.

Once you have the certificate files on your local machine, you will need to install an OpenVPN client application on your computer. If you're on a Windows machine, you can download the installer from the OpenVPN site (*http://openvpn.net/index.php/down load/community-downloads.html*) directly. If you're using a Mac, then I would recommend using a program called Tunnelblick (*http://code.google.com/p/tunnelblick/wiki/ DownloadsEntry*). In either case, be sure to have the manual handy for this next step.

The last step in getting set up is to put the certificate files in the place specified in the client docs and to create a connection configuration file. In the directory specified by the client software user manual, create a file named *MyConnection.ovpn*. There are tons of options for OpenVPN, but in this case you will need to paste only the following into the file.

```
# This is a client profile.
client

# We want to tunnel packets (rather than Ethernet bridging).
dev tun

# Use TCP instead of UDP.
proto tcp

# This is the VPN server we're connecting to.
# Be sure to change this value to YOUR Elastic IP address.
remote vpn.dkrdomain.com 443

# These are the crypto certificates we'll be using.
ca ca.crt
cert client.crt
key client.key
```

```
# Use LZO compression on the channel.
comp-lzo
```

The only thing you need to change from this listing is the hostname that is italicized; that needs to be the IP address of your Elastic IP. You might potentially need to change the name of the *.key* and *.crt* files, too, if you used a name other than *client* when you ran `build-key.bat`. Other than that you're ready to go!

 Make sure that the *.ovpn* configuration file you just created is in the same place as the three certificate files you got earlier. Consult the help for your particular client to find out where that should be. As long as they are all colocated, everything should work on the first go.

Tidying Up and Connecting for the First Time

Before we can connect for the first time we have a little more housekeeping to take care of.

The VPN is set up to communicate over the standard SSL port (443), so we need to make sure that our default security rule allows incoming traffic on that port. As before, click the Security Groups link on the left side of the VPC tab. Highlight the default rule, click the Inbound tab at the bottom of the screen, enter the value **443** for the port, click Add Rule, and then Apply Rule Changes.

You should now see that a new rule allowing incoming traffic on port 443 (HTTPS) is part of the default security group.

While you're there, you should delete the rule allowing RDP traffic, since we want to allow any communication with the infrastructure to occur only through the VPN channel on port 443.

Figure 1-16. The correctly configured security group

Now it's time to test our VPN connection!

Go ahead and select Connect (or something similar) from your VPN client program. You may see a log output scroll across the screen that looks like the following:

```
2012-04-07 11:51:12 Attempting to establish TCP connection with
[AF_INET]107.21.40.175:443 [nonblock]
2012-04-07 11:51:12 MANAGEMENT: >STATE:1333813872,TCP_CONNECT,,,
```

2012-04-07 11:51:13 TCP connection established with [AF_INET]107.21.40.175:443

```
2012-04-07 11:51:13 TCPv4_CLIENT link local: [undef]
2012-04-07 11:51:13 TCPv4_CLIENT link remote: [AF_INET]107.21.40.175:443
2012-04-07 11:51:13 MANAGEMENT: >STATE:1333813873,WAIT,,,
2012-04-07 11:51:13 MANAGEMENT: >STATE:1333813873,AUTH,,,
2012-04-07 11:51:13 TLS: Initial packet from [AF_INET]107.21.40.175:443, sid=ab1e047f
de8e819b
```

**2012-04-07 11:51:14 VERIFY OK: depth=1, C=US, ST=VA, L=Haymarket, O=DKRDomain, OU=IT,
CN=DKRDomain, name=Dave Rensin, emailAddress=dave@dkrdomain.com**
**2012-04-07 11:51:14 VERIFY OK: depth=0, C=US, ST=VA, L=Haymarket, O=DKRDomain, OU=IT,
CN=DKRDomain, name=Dave Rensin, emailAddress=dave@dkrdomain.com**

```
2012-04-07 11:51:15 Data Channel Encrypt: Cipher 'BF-CBC' initialized with 128 bit key
2012-04-07 11:51:15 Data Channel Encrypt: Using 160 bit message hash 'SHA1' for HMAC
authentication
2012-04-07 11:51:15 Data Channel Decrypt: Cipher 'BF-CBC' initialized with 128 bit key
2012-04-07 11:51:15 Data Channel Decrypt: Using 160 bit message hash 'SHA1' for HMAC
authentication
2012-04-07 11:51:15 Control Channel: TLSv1, cipher TLSv1/SSLv3 DHE-RSA-AES256-SHA,
1024 bit RSA
2012-04-07 11:51:15 [DKRDomain] Peer Connection Initiated with
[AF_INET]107.21.40.175:443
2012-04-07 11:51:16 MANAGEMENT: >STATE:1333813876,GET_CONFIG,,,
2012-04-07 11:51:17 SENT CONTROL [DKRDomain]: 'PUSH_REQUEST' (status=1)
2012-04-07 11:51:17 PUSH: Received control message: 'PUSH_REPLY,route
10.8.0.1,topology net30,ping 10,ping-restart 120,ifconfig 10.8.0.6 10.8.0.5'
2012-04-07 11:51:17 OPTIONS IMPORT: timers and/or timeouts modified
2012-04-07 11:51:17 OPTIONS IMPORT: --ifconfig/up options modified
2012-04-07 11:51:17 OPTIONS IMPORT: route options modified
2012-04-07 11:51:17 ROUTE_GATEWAY 192.168.50.1/255.255.255.0 IFACE=en0
HWADDR=58:55:ca:f2:f4:df
2012-04-07 11:51:17 TUN/TAP device /dev/tun0 opened
2012-04-07 11:51:17 do_ifconfig, tt->ipv6=0, tt->did_ifconfig_ipv6_setup=0
2012-04-07 11:51:17 MANAGEMENT: >STATE:1333813877,ASSIGN_IP,,10.8.0.6,
2012-04-07 11:51:17 /sbin/ifconfig tun0 delete
                                      ifconfig: ioctl (SIOCDIFADDR): Can't assign
requested address
2012-04-07 11:51:17 NOTE: Tried to delete pre-existing tun/tap instance -- No Problem
if failure
2012-04-07 11:51:17 /sbin/ifconfig tun0 10.8.0.6 10.8.0.5 mtu 1500 netmask
255.255.255.255 up
2012-04-07 11:51:17 /Applications/Tunnelblick.app/Contents/Resources/
client.up.tunnelblick.sh -m -w -d -atDASNGWrdasngw tun0 1500 1544 10.8.0.6 10.8.0.5
init
2012-04-07 11:51:19 *Tunnelblick client.up.tunnelblick.sh: No network configuration
changes need to be made.
2012-04-07 11:51:19 *Tunnelblick client.up.tunnelblick.sh: Will NOT monitor for other
network configuration changes.
2012-04-07 11:51:19 *Tunnelblick: Flushed the DNS cache
```

```
2012-04-07 11:51:19 MANAGEMENT: >STATE:1333813879,ADD_ROUTES,,,
2012-04-07 11:51:19 /sbin/route add -net 10.8.0.1 10.8.0.5 255.255.255.255
                                    add net 10.8.0.1: gateway 10.8.0.5
2012-04-07 11:51:19 Initialization Sequence Completed

2012-04-07 11:51:19 MANAGEMENT: >STATE:1333813879,CONNECTED,SUCCESS,
10.8.0.6,107.21.40.175
```

In this listing there are four important lines to look for. I've highlighted them to make it easier to spot them.

- The first boldface line shows that there was a successful TCP connection between the VPN client software and the server you've just finished setting up. This tells you that the work you did assigning the Elastic IP is working correctly.
- The next two boldface lines show that there was a successful exchange of cryptographic keys (the certificates) between the server and the client.
- The final boldface line shows that the tunnel was successfully set up and that the client machine now has the IP address of 10.8.0.6.

To test that everything is working well, open up your RDP client and use the IP address of 10.8.0.1 for the server address and try to get a remote desktop connection to the VPN server.

If that works you're all set!

 The server is preconfigured to give your computer an IP address in the 10.8.0.x range. The server will *always* be reachable at the address 10.8.0.1 as long as the VPN connection is active.

Your New Topology

From this point forward, whenever you want to do maintenance on any of the machines in your new VPC you will have to:

1. Establish a VPN connection.
2. RDP to 10.8.0.1.
3. Connect to the other instances in your VPC from there.

You'll get the hang of this quickly enough in the next chapter.

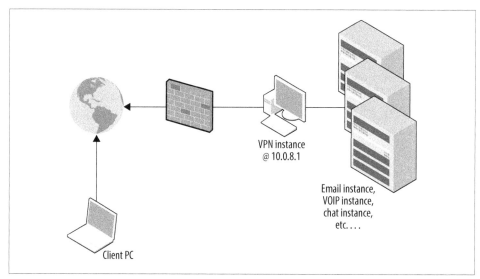

Figure 1-17. Network topology of your VPC

Wrapping Up

Congratulations!

You've just done some of the hardest stuff in the whole book. Your virtual private cloud is set up and you now have a rock-solid secure VPN connection with which to reach it. In the following chapters you'll explore the details of setting up various IT services you'll need (such as email, chat, and voice). For now, though, you should be content in the knowledge that you have accomplished in probably less than an hour what would normally have taken the better part of two days.

Next stop, Active Directory and the Primary Domain Controller!

Directories, Controllers, and Authorities—Oh My!

Here in Chapter 2 you're going to set up the guts of your infrastructure—the plumbing that makes it all go. By the time you're done you'll have:

- A new Windows domain and corresponding Primary Domain Controller (PDC)
- An instance of Active Directory to keep track of the users and computers in your domain
- Your own root certificate authority (CA) so you can issue security certificates for certain services like email.

Ready?

Let's go!

So Young for Such a Big Promotion!

The VPN server you set up in the last chapter won't likely be overburdened by incoming connections most of the time. So, in an attempt at economy you'll make it dual-purpose and have it also be the Primary Domain Controller (PDC), Active Directory Server (AD), and root certificate authority (CA).

Windows networks are collections of machines, users, and groups. The machine that keeps track of all those things is our primary Active Directory Server (AD). In earlier times, the primary AD was a different machine than the PDC. As of late, though, it's been commonplace to make them the same machine.

For this book that's exactly what you're going to do.

Right now you have a brand-new machine dedicated to the purpose of being a VPN server. It's a perfectly fine job to do, but a bit of a waste of its potential. In this section you will:

1. Give it a permanent name.
2. Promote it to be your principle AD server.
3. Make it the primary DNS server for your other VPC instances.

Changing the Name

First things first: connect via the VPN and connect via RDP to 10.8.0.1.

Instances created in Amazon EC2 automatically have a unique name assigned to them. That's all well and good, but you really want your instances to have names that mean something. For example, you might want your combo VPN/AD instance to have a meaningful name like *Gateway*.

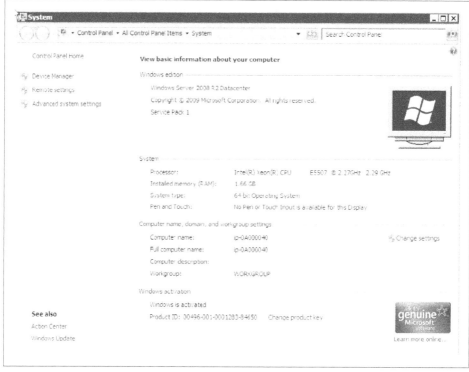

Figure 2-1. The default name for your VPN instance

Right-clicking My Computer and selecting Properties gives you the figure above. As you can see, the machine name IP-0A000040 is not exactly brimming with meaning. To change the machine name, you first have to configure the EC2 tools on the instance to not automatically name the machine. If you click the Start menu, you will see a utility named *EC2ConfigService Settings*.

Figure 2-2. The Start menu

On the screen that comes up, uncheck the box labeled Set Computer Name and click OK. Now you're free to rename the instance to whatever you like. In this case you want to change its name from IP-0A000040 to Gateway. The easiest way to do this is to open a command prompt and type the following:

```
netdom renamecomputer IP-0A000040 /NewName:Gateway
```

You should, of course remember to substitute the name of *your* instance and the name you want to give it.

The changes won't take effect until after you reboot the instance, so go ahead and do that. Just wait until your VPN connection software tells you that it has re-established its link. Then you can go ahead and re-RDP back into the instance.

Promoting the Instance to an Active Directory Server

On the lower left-hand corner of the VPN server's desktop you will see the icon for the Server Manager. Go ahead and click it; the main Server Manager window should open.

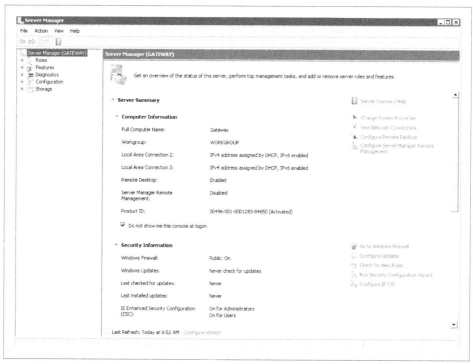

Figure 2-3. The main Server Manager window

A server can have several roles. In this case, you want the server to have the *Active Directory Domain Services* role. On the left side of the current window, click the Roles item. You should see in the main pane that there are currently no roles configured for this server. Click the Add Roles link in the main pane, and click Next to skip to the next screen. You should now be presented with a list of roles to add to the server.

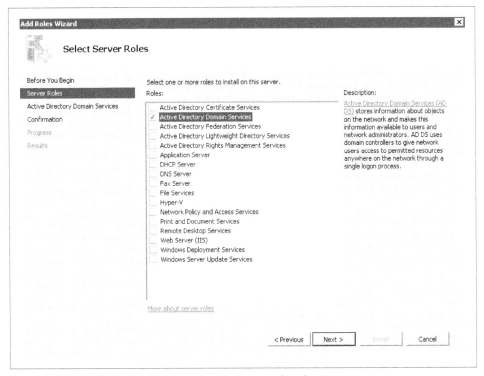

Figure 2-4. Select the Active Directory Domain Service role only

Select *only* the Active Directory Domain Services role, and then click Next. Click Next again and then click Install.

After a few moments the installation will complete, and you will be prompted with the following screen:

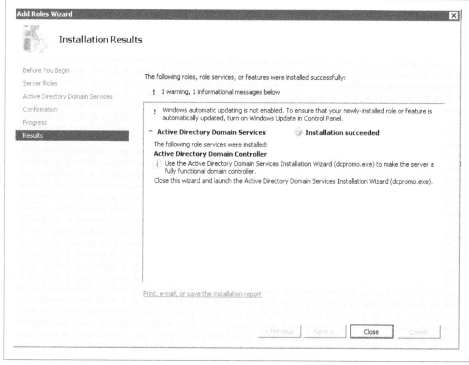

Figure 2-5. Promoting the server to a domain controller

This next step is very important. *Do not select the Close button!* Instead, click "Close the wizard and launch the Active Directory Domain Services Installation Wizard (dcpromo.exe)."

Follow these steps exactly and all will be good.

1. In the Welcome window of the AD Domain Services Installation Wizard, click Next.

2. Click Next again on the Operating Systems Compatibility page.

3. On the Choose a Deployment Configuration page select "Create a new domain in a new forest" and select Next.

   You should now be on the Name the Forest Root Domain page, where you will name your AD domain. You should be aware of some common practices. Let's say, for example, you registered the domain *MyCompany.com* back in Chapter 1. The convention would be for you to name your AD domain *MyCompany.local* or *MyCompany.internal*. Both are common. Since the public domain name I created was *DKRDomain.com*, I'm going to use the value *dkrdomain.local*.

4. After you fill in your choice, select Next.

The wizard will take a few moments to verify that the new AD forest name is not already in use and that the name you picked is valid for the NetBIOS protocol. Just give it a minute or two...

The wizard should now present you with the Set Forest Functional Level page.

5. Change the value in the drop-down to *Windows Server 2008 R2* and click Next.

The wizard will take another couple of minutes or so to examine the DNS configuration. That's normal. Just sit tight and let it run.

6. Now that the Active Directory Domain Service role has been installed, you will be prompted to install the DNS Server role, too, from the Additional Domain Controller Options screen. Go ahead and just click Next.

If you've followed these steps correctly, then you should see the following error:

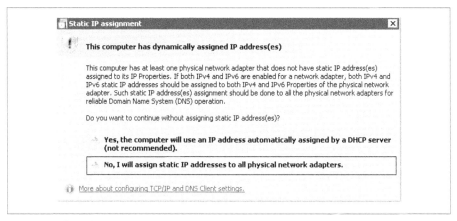

Figure 2-6. Static IP warning

7. Please pay close attention here. It is *very* important that you select "Yes, the computer will use an IP address automatically assigned by a DHCP server." Never mind that it's "not recommended." You need this particular configuration to make things work smoothly in your VPC. I'll get into more detail about this in just a bit, but for now just click Yes.

8. Click Yes on the screen that asks "Do you wish to continue?"

9. Accept the defaults presented in the Location for Database, Log Files, and SYSVOL window by clicking Next.

10. The next screen will prompt you for directory services restore password. You can, of course, use any password you like. For the sake of administrative simplicity, I would use the password you selected for your Administrator account back in Chapter 1. Fill it in and select Next.

11. Finally, go ahead and select Next on the summary page.

The wizard will apply all the changes you approved. This process can take as little as 1 minute or as long as 10 minutes. In any case, just let it run.

12. Click the Finish button when the wizard is done, then reboot the instance when prompted.

A Few Words About DNS and DHCP

Since the instance is rebooting, this would be a good time to talk about how DNS and DHCP normally work versus how you'll need to make them work in your VPC.

The "normal"

In a normal installation of a Windows IT infrastructure (where the physical machines are all in one location, like your office) it is customary to make the primary AD server not only a DNS server, but a DHCP server too.

 Dynamic Host Control Protocol (DHCP) is what most kinds of computers (Windows, Mac, Linux, etc.) use to get assigned their IP address, the address of the DNS servers they should use, and the routing information they need to get to the rest of the network and the Internet.

DHCP is super handy because it means your don't have to manually configure each machine in your infrastructure. Since you always want your AD server and your DNS server to know the IP addresses of the machines on your network, it makes good sense to install all three services on the same box. This configuration lets you address a specific machine by its hostname (e.g., *mycomputer.dkrdomain.local*) instead of having to remember its IP address.

The "new normal"

Virtual infrastructures like an Amazon VPC almost always provide a DHCP service for you. You *can* disable it, but that's more trouble than it's worth. Instead, the right way to integrate it into the infrastructure you just configured is to change its key parameters to marry up nicely with your machines.

You might also recall that when you installed the AD server role, the wizard complained that your new AD machine wasn't using a static IP address. I told you to ignore the warning and leave it using the DHCP provided by Amazon in the VPC.

Why?

One of the many neat things about an Amazon VPC is that its DHCP service is *guaranteed* to always provide the same IP address to its member instances. That means if your new AD server has an internal Amazon address of 10.0.0.209, it will *always* get that IP address—no matter how many times it gets rebooted. For all intents and purposes this means that it really *does* have a static IP address.

Configuring the Default VPC DHCP to Play Nice with Your New Domain

Now that you understand a bit more about the default topology of a VPC, it's time to reconfigure how Amazon assigns DHCP settings to your machines. Specifically, you want the VPC to automatically tell subsequent instances the following things:

- The default DNS machine for the VPC should be the AD server you just configured, and not the current VPC default.
- The current VPC default should be demoted to the fallback DNS server for any new machines.
- All new machines should be able to perform WINS (Windows Name Service) requests to your new AD server.

Before you can make these changes, though, you have to note a couple of key pieces of information. The most important of these is the internal IP address that Amazon has assigned to your gateway instance. The easiest way to find this is to look in the EC2 tab of the AWS Management Console.

Figure 2-7. Getting the internal IP address of the server

In this case you can see that your server has been allocated the address 10.0.0.209.

The next two pieces of information you need are the IP address of the default gateway for the VPC and the IP address for the default DNS server for the VPC. Fortunately, once you know the internal IP address of just one machine in the VPC, you can easily figure out the other two. The default gateway *always* ends in .1 and the default DNS *always* ends in .2. So in this case, since your machine is on the 10.0.0.x subnet, that means

- The default gateway address is 10.0.0.1
- The default VPC DNS is 10.0.0.2

Armed with these three pieces of information, you can reconfigure the VPC to play nice with your new domain.

Changing the VPC DHCP Option Set

The rules governing the information that the VPC DHCP server hands out are contained in a record called a *DHCP Option Set*. These records are found by clicking the DHCP Option Sets link on the VPC tab in the console.

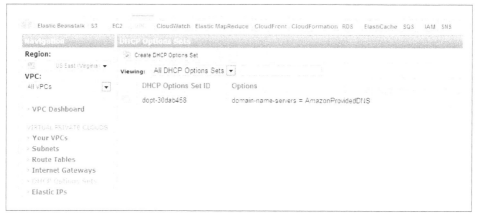

Figure 2-8. The Default DHCP option set

The default rule just says that every machine that gets its DHCP information from the VPC should set its DNS to the Amazon-provided value. In the case of the VPC that I set up, that would be 10.0.0.2. But you're looking for something a bit more robust. You want every new instance to look first at your AD server (10.0.0.209) and then at the default 10.0.0.2 address. You also want all of your machines to have a default DNS suffix equal to the domain name you chose earlier. Since I chose *dkdomain.local*, that's what I want appended to each new hostname. For example, if I create a new machine instance and name it *Chat*, I want it to be addressable inside my VPC as *chat.dkrdomain* *.local*.

To accomplish these things, you need to create a new DHCP Options Set.

First, click the Create DHCP Options Set button at the top of the frame. You will be greeted with the following:

Figure 2-9. A blank option set

Using the values you calculated earlier, fill in this window. Please be sure to use *your* values; don't just repeat the example values I'm using here!

Figure 2-10. The completed option set

Please note that in the "domain name servers" field you should enter the IP address of your machine *plus* the special value *AmazonProvidedDNS*—separated by a comma. When you're done just click Yes, Create. You should now see two option sets in your list: the default set and the new set you just created.

The next thing you need to do is to change the option set being used by our VPC from the default set to the new set.

1. Click the Your VPCs link.
2. Right-click the VPC and select Change DHCP Option Set.
3. Choose the set you just created from the drop-down.
4. Select Yes, Change.
5. Click the DHCP Option Sets link on the left side of the window.
6. Select the default option set and delete it by clicking the Delete button and selecting Yes, Delete.

Now, every time you create a new instance in the VPC it will get the DNS, NetBIOS, and domain options you have just configured.

Reconnecting with RDP

Go ahead and reconnect to the VPN and then connect to the machine via RDP. You might notice that the credentials you were using earlier no longer work!

Not to worry.

When you converted the VPN server to an AD domain controller you changed the username under which you need to log in. Instead of the old name of *<MachineName> \Administrator*, we'll now need to use the login name of *<DomainName>\Administrator*.

For example, my machine is named Gateway and I used to log in with the name *Gateway \Administrator*. Now, however, I've created a domain named *dkrdomain.local*, so I now have to use the name *dkrdomain\Administrator*. (Yes, you can leave off the *.local* part.)

The password will be the same as when you logged in before.

 Before continuing on in this book, please make sure you can successfully login to the VPN machine using the new domain username and old password. Seriously, unless you can accomplish that, you can't progress much farther in this book.

Creating Your Own Certificate Authority

From time to time it will be important for you to be able to issue your own security certificates—when enabling encryption via SSL for email or Web, for example. In order to gain this capability, there is one more role you need to add to our server: *Active Directory Certificate Services*.

1. Open the Server Manager, highlight Roles, and select Add Roles.
2. Select Next on the Before You Begin page and check the box marked Active Directory Certificate Services.

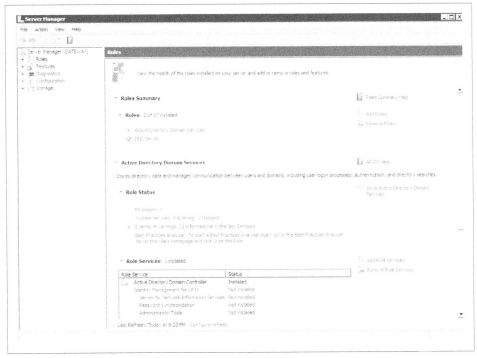

Figure 2-11. Opening the Server Manager

3. Click Next.

4. Click Next again on the *AD CS* page.

5. On the Role Services page select only Certification Authority and click Next.

6. We want an Enterprise instance (rather than a standalone instance), so leave the setting as is on the Setup Type page and click Next.

7. We also want a root CA rather than a subordinate CA, so you can just click Next again.

8. Since this is the first root CA in this domain, you need to create a new private key. Once again, Next.

9. Leave the default cryptography settings alone on the Cryptography page, and hit our old pal the Next button again.

The CA name is also fine as is. Continue on.

10. Five years is a plenty long time for a certificate, so you can leave this setting alone. You can, of course, tweak it any way you want. When you're done, move along.

11. There's nothing to do on the Certificate Database page, so keep going.

12. You should be happy with your settings, so now it's time to click Install.

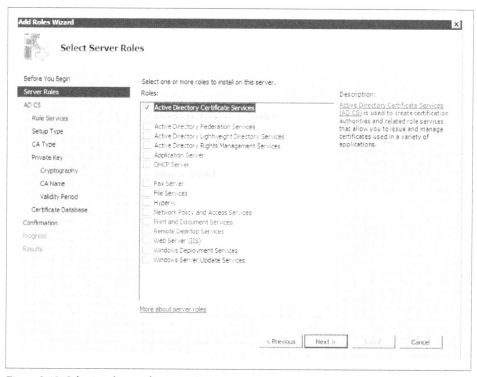

Figure 2-12. Selecting the certificate services

Sixty seconds or so later you should see the following message:

Figure 2-13. Time to run Windows Update

Notice that the installer seems to be a bit grumpy because you haven't enabled Windows Update, yet. It's a good point, so do that now.

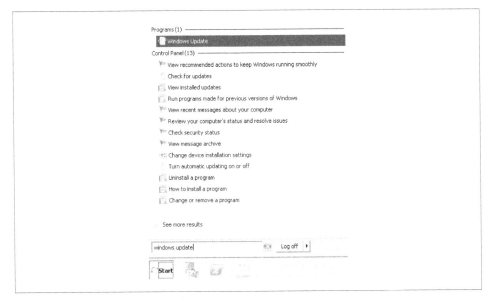

Figure 2-14. Starting Windows Update

1. Click the Start menu and type **Windows Update**. Then select the first item that pops up.
2. On the screen that comes up, click the link titled Change Settings.
3. Select "Install updates automatically" from the drop-down and click OK.
4. Go ahead and opt to install any important *and* optional updates, and let the updater do its thing. Since this is the first update after the new instance was installed, this process might take a while. Now's a good time to grab a coffee, read a book, change your oil, etc.
5. Finally, when the system says it needs to restart in order to apply the changes (it almost *always* says that), go ahead and let it.

Wrapping Up

Whew! This has been a busy 20 or so pages.

You've successfully promoted your VPN server to a full-blown Active Directory Server —including both DNS and Domain Services. You've reconfigured our VPC to play nicely with the expected DHCP and DNS for your newly created domain, and you've even set up your own root CA so you can issue your very own test certificates.

Your next project will be setting up and configuring your own Microsoft Exchange email server. (The fun just keeps coming, doesn't it?)

## CHAPTER 3

Let There Be Email!

Now that you have the domain, Active Directory, and VPN services configured, it's time to set up email. For the purposes of this book, I'm going to walk through installing a Microsoft Exchange Server instance in the VPC. You can, of course, use other email solutions, but Exchange is by far the most widely used email platform in corporations of any size.

"Why am I setting up email first?" you might ask.

That's easy. It's the one service absolutely *everybody* in *any* IT infrastructure uses all the time. Some services can go up or come down from time to time, but when email is down *everybody* complains. (Often by trying to send email messages to the IT department, ironically enough.)

Setting Up the Instance

Before you can go about installing the Exchange Server software, you first have to stand up a suitable instance in the VPC. Before you can even do *that*, you need to prepare the network a little. In this case you need to create a new, empty, security group and assign it to your VPC. You're not going to do anything with this new group just yet, but you need to have it ready. Its purpose will be to hold the firewall rules that apply *only* to your Exchange server. Go ahead and create a new security group from the VPC tab and name it **Exchange Server**.

Now it's time to bring up a new instance to host your Exchange server. Go ahead and use the Quick Start wizard to set up a regular Windows 2008 R2 Server, but make sure it has Internet Information Services (IIS) with it. You'll need that a little later.

Figure 3-1. New security group

Figure 3-2. Your new AMI

Once again, you'll need an instance size of m1.small, and you will need to make sure that the new server is created in your VPC.

 Here's a mistake I've made plenty of times. I create a new server instance and *forget* to put it in my VPC! Once the server comes up, there's no way to migrate into the VPC, so all I can do is terminate it and start again. The point here is to always go slow and make sure you've looked over every option. In this case, the dictum *measure twice, cut once* really applies.

Figure 3-3. Instance details

Figure 3-4. Pick your security groups

While you're in the instance details, you need to edit the security settings and make sure that the new instance has both the "default" and Exchange Server security groups associated with it. In fact, every server you create in this book will *always* have at least the *default* group, since that group holds the rule that allows each of your servers to talk to each other.

When you're done editing your settings, they should look like the following:

Create a New Instance   Cancel ✕

Microsoft Windows Server 2008 R2 with SQL Server Express and IIS (ami-eb8c5482)
Platform: Windows   Microsoft Windows Server 2008 R2 SP1 Datacenter edition, 64-bit architecture, Microsoft
Architecture: x86_64   SQLServer 2008 Express, Internet Information Services 7, ASP.NET 3.5.

Please review your settings and click **Launch** to finish or **Edit details** to make changes.
Instance Details
                    Name: Exchange   Type: m1.small
    Detailed Monitoring: No   Availability Zone: us-east-1a
    Shutdown Behaviour: Stop   Termination Protection: No
    Launch into a VPC: Yes (subnet-8aafcce2)

Security Details
                Key Pair: dkr-ec2   Security Groups: default, Exchange_Server

Advanced Details
              Kernel ID: Default   Ramdisk ID: Default
    Instance Tenancy: default
              User Data:

                                                                      Edit details   Launch

‹ Go Back

Figure 3-5. Final settings

Click Launch to start up the new host. This will take a few minutes, so you should get some other stuff out of the way while you are waiting.

Since your new Exchange server is going to have to talk to the outside world in order to transfer email in and out, you'll need to allocate a new public IP address to it. From the VPC tab, allocate a new Elastic IP (EIP) address.

 Just like when you brought up your new server instance, you *must* be sure that the EIP address you reserve is for your VPC and is not a generic EC2 address. If you make sure you allocate the EIP address from the VPC tab in the console, you won't have any problems.

Figure 3-6. Allocate a new EIP

At this point you'll need to wait a few minutes until your new server instance is marked as running in your list of instances. This list self-refreshes, so there's nothing to do but wait. Now is as a good a time as any for a bio break/coffee run/soda injection.

When your new server is finally showing as running in the instance list, you need to assign your new EIP to it.

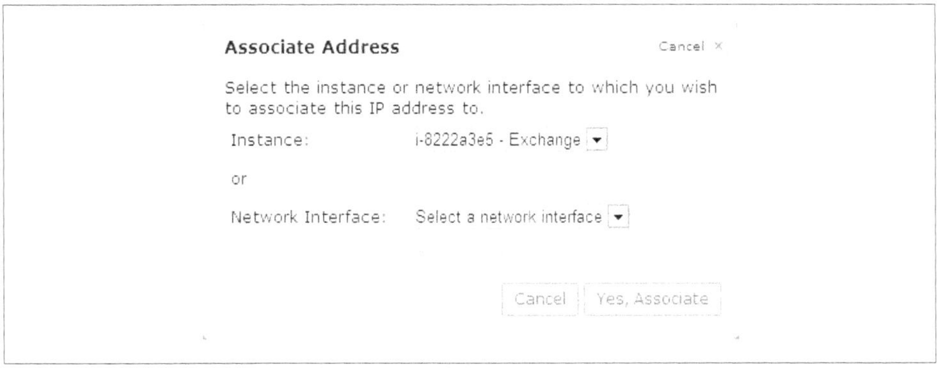

Figure 3-7. Assign the EIP

At this point, take a moment to consider your current network security configuration. Your new server instance has two security groups associated to it: default and Exchange Server. The default group allows any other instance that belongs to the same group to freely exchange packets on any port with any other host in the group. You need this so that all the machines inside your VPC are free to talk to each other in whatever way is required to function correctly.

The second thing to remember is that the other security group to which your new instance belongs—Exchange Server—currently allows *no* inbound traffic whatsoever. (That'll change later.) For now, though, the upshot of these two facts is that there is no way to RDP to your new server from an outside IP address in order to configure it!

This is by design.

In order to touch *any* machine inside your VPC you have to

1. Get the *internal* IP address of the machine you want to connect to
2. Connect to your VPC via the VPN connection you created earlier
3. RDP to the VPN machine (named Gateway in your case)
4. RDP again from Gateway to your new host

Now, I know what you're thinking: "Man, this VPN/double RDP thingy is kind of a hassle!"

Yes, yes it is ... And that's a good thing.

RDP is not a very secure protocol and is periodically hacked (and then patched by Microsoft). For this reason we absolutely do not want to be able to RDP to any machine in the VPC—including the Gateway—from an outside IP address. The proper way to secure your network is to be required to *first* VPN in to your VPC and *then* RDP in to your desired machine. In fact, while writing this book I received the following email from Amazon:

> Dear EC2 Customer,
>
> In your continuing effort to ensure the security of your customers, we want to make you aware of a recent Microsoft security announcement and how it may affect you. Microsoft has announced a vulnerability in the Remote Desktop Protocol (RDP) affecting all supported versions of the Windows operating system (CVE-2012-0173). RDP allows users to administer Windows systems in a manner that displays the remote Windows desktop locally. This vulnerability may allow an attacker to gain remote access to Windows-based systems or deny access to RDP. NOTE: This vulnerability is distinct from the RDP vulnerability announced by Microsoft on March 12, 2012 (CVE-2012-0002).
>
> Detailed information about the vulnerability, including Microsoft instructions for updating to address this vulnerability, is available here:
>
> http://technet.microsoft.com/en-us/security/bulletin/ms12-036
>
> AWS customers running Windows instances, and who have enabled the automatic software updating feature within Windows, should download and install the necessary update which will subsequently address this vulnerability automatically. Instructions on how to ensure automatic updating is enabled are here:
>
> http://windows.microsoft.com/en-US/windows/help/windows-update
>
> AWS customers running Windows instances, and who have not enabled the automatic software updating feature within Windows, should manually install the necessary update by following the instructions here:
>
> http://windows.microsoft.com/en-US/windows/help/windows-update
>
> Microsoft provides additional guidance about automatic software update configuration options for Windows here:
>
> http://support.microsoft.com/kb/294871

We also want to make you aware of one or more of your security groups that you have
configured to allow RDP access from the Internet. This may increase your exposure to
this type of vulnerability. Specifically, we suggest that you examine the following
security groups:

Region - Security Group
_____

US East (Virginia) - quicklaunch-1

In order to limit the exposure of your instances to this type of vulnerability, AWS
strongly recommends that you restrict inbound TCP port 3389 to only those syource IP
addresses from which legitimate RDP sessions should originate. These access
restrictions can be applied by configuring your EC2 Security Groups accordingly. For
information and examples on how to properly configure and apply Security Groups, please
refer to the following documentation:

http://docs.amazonwebservices.com/AWSEC2/latest/UserGuide/index.html?adding-security-
group-rules.html

If you need additional assistance, documentation related to security best practices
may be found at http://aws.amazon.com/security/ .

Regards,

The Amazon Web Services Team

This message was produced and distributed by Amazon Web Services LLC, 410 Terry Avenue
North, Seattle, Washington 98109-5210

See, even Amazon agrees with me! <grin>

The other thing to note is that the way you've configured your VPN allows you to get
just to the Gateway machine, and no further.

This is another security precaution that guarantees that even if the VPN is hacked, and
even if the password for the Gateway machine is hacked, an attacker *still* will need to
hack the password of the Exchange Server to gain access.

So, in order to administer the Exchange Server, you first have to connect via the VPN,
then RDP to the gateway, and finally RDP from the gateway to the Exchange server.

Referring back to Step 1 above, you first have to get the *internal* IP address of your new
server. You can get this from the details page about the instance.

The next thing you need to do before you can connect to the new instance is to get its
machine-generated password. Brand-new stock Windows AMIs all have their passwords autogencrated when they first boot. To connect to them, you need to get that
password from Amazon. To do this, right-click the instance and select Get Windows
Password and get your temporary Windows password.

Figure 3-8. Get the internal IP of the new instance

Figure 3-9. Get the machine password

Next, establish a VPN connection to your gateway machine and RDP into it as before. Once you RDP into your gateway machine, click the Start button and type

`mstsc /console /v:<the internal ip address of the exchange server>`.

Figure 3-10. RDP in to the Exchange Server

Now use the temporary password you just retrieved to log in to the Exchange box as Administrator.

 Be sure to use a '\' in front of the username Administrator, so RDP knows you want to connect as the administrator of the local machine.

As you've done previously, you want to change the name of the machine from the default Amazon name to something more meaningful. There should already be a link to the EC2 Service Properties on your desktop (or in the Start menu under Programs). In the EC2 Service Properties, you want to uncheck the Set Computer Name option. This prevents the machine from reverting to its default name on reboot. Also, make sure that the machine *is not* set to reset the password on the next reboot.

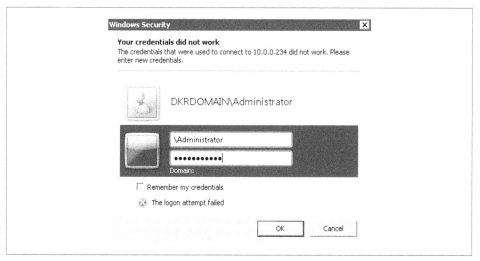

Figure 3-11. Logging in

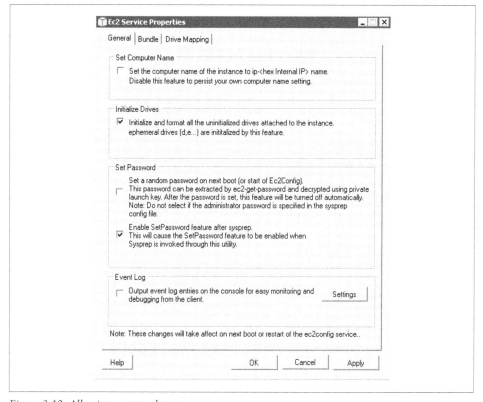

Figure 3-12. Allowing a name change

Now you should change the name of the machine. Click the Start menu, right-click Computer, and select Properties. Finally, click the Change Settings link on the page.

Figure 3-13. Time to change the name and add it to the workgroup

Now, give the machine a memorable name (I used *Exchange* for mine) and add it to the domain we created in the last chapter—in my case it was *dkrdomain.local*.

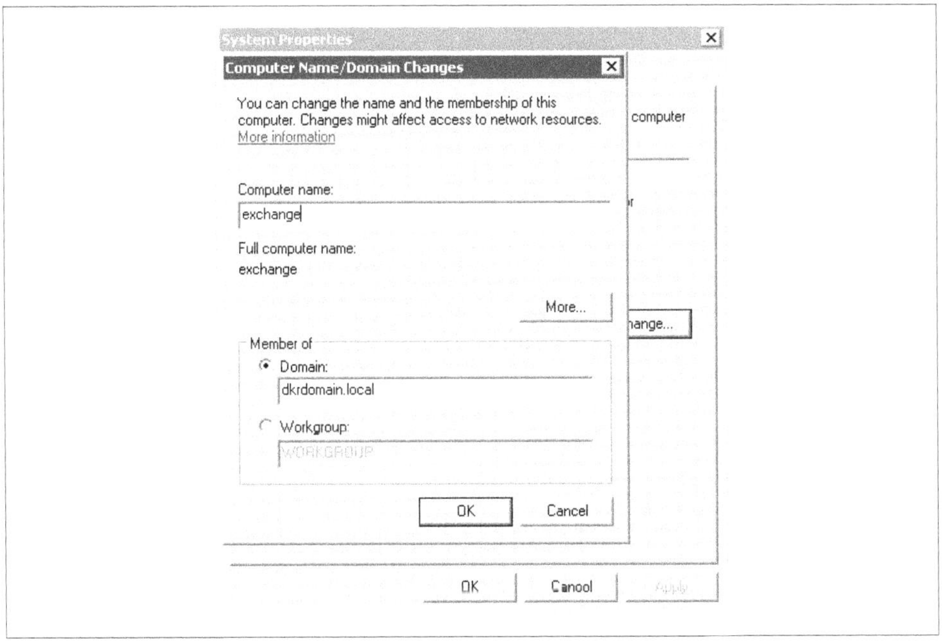

Figure 3-14. Setting the new name

When prompted, be certain to use the username and password for the domain administrator you set up in the last chapter.

Figure 3-15. Credentialing to the domain

If all goes as it should, you should get a very nice welcome message.

Figure 3-16. Welcome to the domain

Installing Exchange

With your instance up, running, and in your domain, you can now install Exchange Server. For the sake of cost and expediency, you are going to install the 120-day free trial edition from the Microsoft site.

Step 1 is to RDP from the gateway machine to your new instance (which we've cleverly named Exchange.)

Figure 3-17. RDP using the new name

You can get the download directly from *http://www.microsoft.com/en-us/download/details.aspx?id=21570*. It's a big download, so it might take a few minutes. Even though

Amazon has a ridiculously fat Internet pipe to its data centers, Microsoft sometimes likes to bandwidth-throttle its downloads depending on the time of day you try.

In any event, make sure you download the actual Exchange 2010 installation file and *not* the also available preconfigured virtual hard drive (VHD).

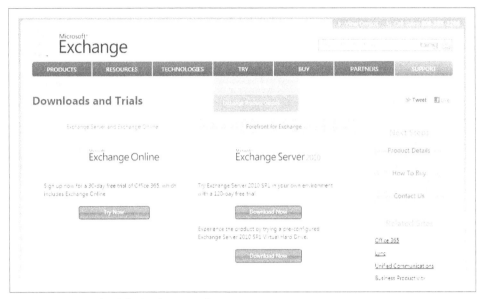

Figure 3-18. Download the Exchange trial

When the download completes, open it and run the setup wizard.

Your first two prerequisites—the .NET framework and Windows PowerShell—should already be installed because of the AMI type we selected earlier. That means the first thing you'll have to do is to pick an installation language.

 This step seems like it should be a no-brainer, but it isn't. In fact, it hosed me big time when I first did it. When you select your language option, be certain to select the option for installing only those languages that come on the DVD—not the ones in the bundle. If you don't do this, you'll have serious problems later and will need to redo the install.

With your language speed bump out of the way, it's time to get on to the main show. The main wizard screen should automatically open when the language options are done.

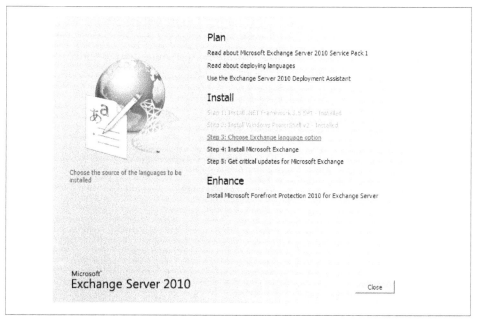

Figure 3-19. Running the wizard

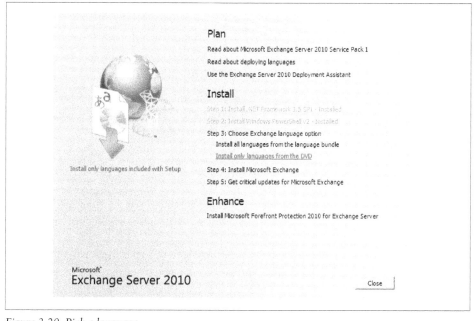

Figure 3-20. Pick a language

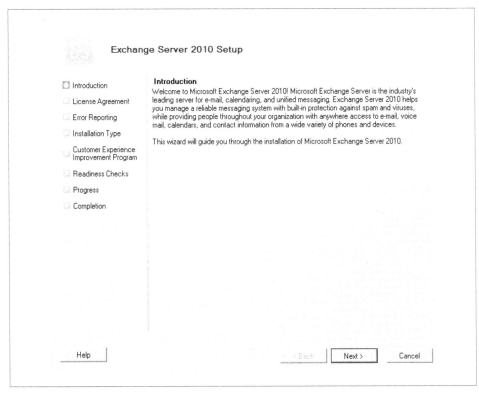

Figure 3-21. The Main wizard

Exchange has somewhere in the neighborhood of a bazillion possible configuration options, and you'll use some of them later. For the meantime, though, when prompted please elect to do a typical Exchange Server installation.

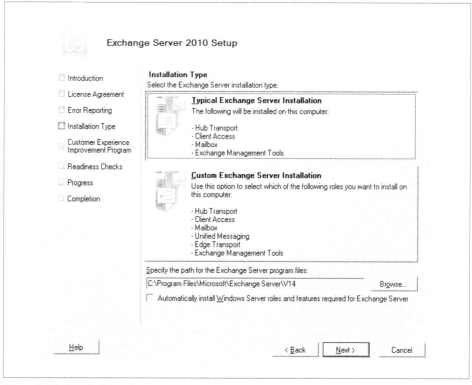

Figure 3-22. A typical install

For the uninitiated, Exchange divides the things it knows about (users, machines, etc.) into *organizations*. In this installation you are only ever going to have one organization, so pick an easy name for your first organization. I picked Our Employees.

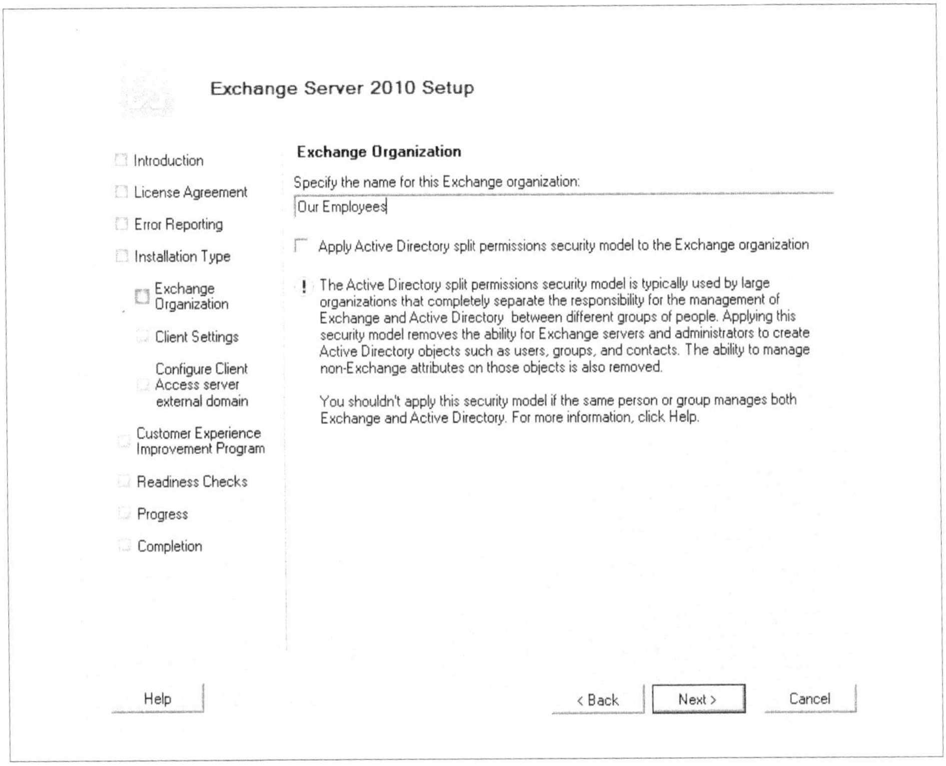

Figure 3-23. First organization

The next decision you face is to specify your *external domain*. In a nutshell, your external domain will be the domain name under which you will be exposing this server to the outside world. For example, my domain is *dkrdomain.com*, and I've decided that my mail server will be named *mail.dkrdomain.com*, so that's the value I used. If your principal domain is going to be something like *supercoolstartup.com*, then that's what you should use.

Once again, this is a "measure twice, cut once" moment. If you screw this up, the server will have a heck of a time sending and receiving email from the outside world!

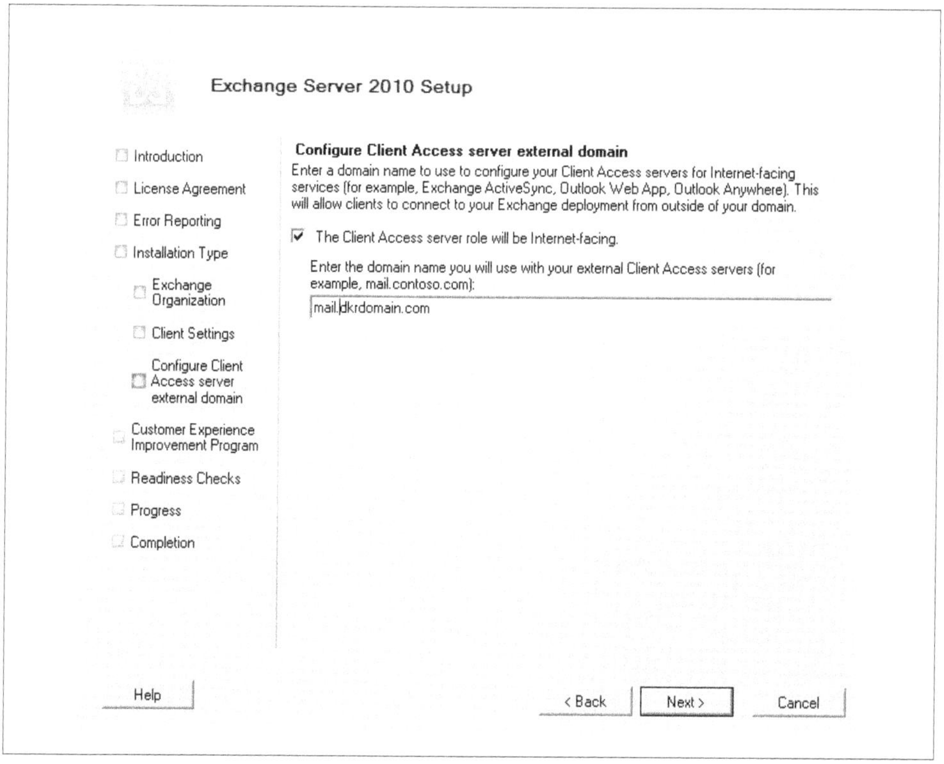

Figure 3-24. External access domain

When you click Next, the installer will start to set up the fabled Microsoft prerequisites.

An Exchange server does a lot of things and has to be available at all times—since email is a mission-critical corporate application. As a software developer, I can tell you from personal experience that those two requirements will make the software ridiculously complex. The more complex the software is when running, the more the environment in which it runs must be set up "just so" in order for things to work properly.

Since Microsoft makes lots of complex corporate business applications—many of which will run on the same machine side by side—they face a particularly thorny challenge in making sure that the operating environment for the software is correct. As a result, there's a good chance that when you install a Microsoft product of any complexity, it will want to check that a number of operating conditions are met *before* it lets you install. These conditions are the infamous Microsoft *prerequisites* and are the stuff of lore in the software industry—mainly because they can be very different between software packages.

Sometimes the software operating conditions need to be very precise in order for the application to run effectively. This can mean that meeting all the prerequisites is more complicated than actually installing the main application.

Not surprisingly, Exchange Server is such an application.

The key piece of advice I will give you is this: *read everything on the prerequisites screens very carefully and do exactly what they tell you to do!*

Just the installer for this software goes through thousands of hours of quality assurance (QA) testing to make sure every conceivable edge case is covered, and that the instructions presented to the user during the prerequisite and installation phases are clear and precise. Follow them to the letter, and life will be good.

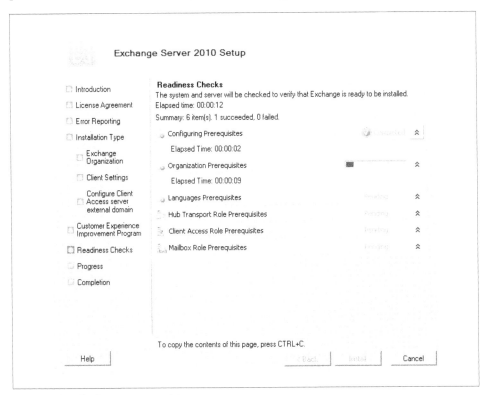

Figure 3-25. The famous prerequisites

The first prerequisite that will fail during your installation has to do with your Active Directory installation. Some of the data structures relating to user accounts and permissions must be expanded in detail in order to accommodate the functions of the Exchange server.

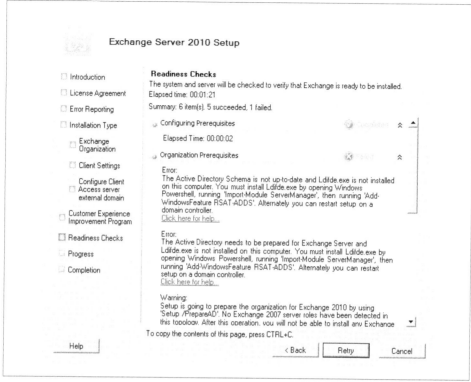

Figure 3-26. The Active Directory configuration is not yet complete

If you wanted to, you could change the required Active Directory permissions and structures by hand. Then again, you could also machine your own metal and silicone and make your own physical server directly from its constituent earth elements.

What? You don't feel like going through all that? You just want to satisfy the prereqs and move on?

Yeah, me too.

The easiest way to get your AD ready is to let the installer mess with it. But your Amazon AMI default installation doesn't have the administrative feature enabled that would let the installer configure AD for you. The easiest way to fix this is by using the Windows PowerShell.

A Quick History of Windows PowerShell

Quoting directly from the Wikipedia (*http://en.wikipedia.org/wiki/Powershell*) article on Windows PowerShell:

> Every released version of Microsoft DOS and Microsoft Windows for personal computers has included a command-line interface tool (shell). These are COM-MAND.COM (in installations relying on MS-DOS, including Windows 9x) and cmd.exe (in Windows NT family operating systems). The shell is a command line interpreter that supports a few basic commands.

> For other purposes, a separate console application must be invoked from the shell. The shell also includes a scripting language (batch files), which can be used to automate various tasks. However, the shell cannot be used to automate all facets of GUI functionality, in part because command-line equivalents of operations exposed via the graphical interface are limited, and the scripting language is elementary and does not allow the creation of complex scripts.

> In Windows Server 2003, the situation was improved, but scripting support was still considered unsatisfactory. Microsoft attempted to address some of these shortcomings by introducing the Windows Script Host in 1998 with Windows 98, and its command-line based host: **cscript.exe**. It integrates with the Active Script engine and allows scripts to be written in compatible languages, such as JScript and VBScript, leveraging the APIs exposed by applications via COM. However, it too has its own deficiencies: it is not integrated with the shell, its documentation is not very accessible, and it quickly gained a reputation as a system vulnerability vector after several high-profile computer viruses exploited weaknesses in its security provisions.

> Different versions of Windows provided various special-purpose command line interpreters (such as **netsh** and WMIC) with their own command sets. None of them were integrated with the command shell; nor were they interoperable. By 2002 Microsoft had started to develop a new approach to command line management, including a shell called Monad (aka Microsoft Shell or MSH). The shell and the ideas behind it were published in August 2002 in a white paper entitled Monad Manifesto. Monad was to be a new extensible command shell with a fresh design that would be capable of automating a full range of core administrative tasks. Microsoft first showed off Monad at the Professional Development Conference in Los Angeles in September 2003.

PowerShell is a superpowerful (no pun intended) command-line environment that lets you do practically everything under the sun—including add or remove features of the operating system.

Click the blue icon two to the right of the Start menu to open PowerShell.

Figure 3-27. PowerShell

Once at a PowerShell prompt, execute the two following commands:

```
Import-Module ServerManager
Add-WindowsFeature RSAT-ADDS
```

The first line adds to the current PowerShell session the ability to manage certain server-level functions. The second line installs the feature Remote Server Administrative Tools —Active Directory Domain Services. This lets trusted users and programs modify the Active Directory configuration for the domain.

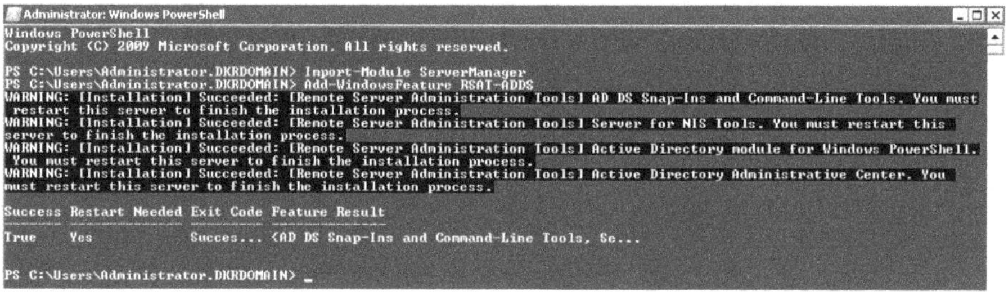

Figure 3-28. Time to reboot

At this point you will need to reboot the instance in order for the feature installation to complete properly. When the instance comes back online, RDP in to it as before and rerun the Exchange Server setup tool. You should see the following message:

Figure 3-29. Continuing on

Click Yes and you are back off to the races.

Eventually, you will encounter two more warnings. The first explains that since setup can't find any other Exchange servers on the network and since Exchange 2010 works differently than previous versions of Exchange, it is going to configure the Active Directory server in such a way that all subsequent Exchange servers installed on the network must be at least version 2010.

This is an interesting tidbit of information to know in case you ever want to install a second server, but for now, ignore it.

The second warning is one you should not ignore. It says that a critical piece of the Exchange Server (the Hub Transport component) is missing certain software components needed to function correctly.

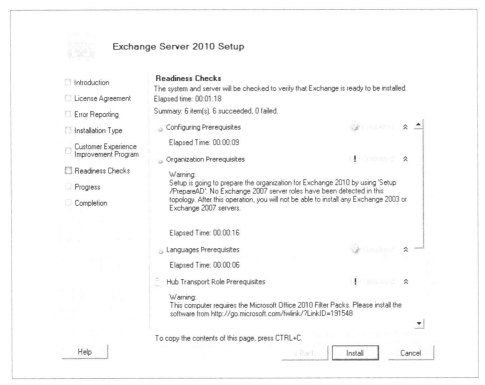

Figure 3-30. Install filter packs, ignore warning

Note that the error very kindly points you to the exact spot on the Microsoft website where you can get the missing software.

 Absolutely, positively, under penalty of death, make sure you download and install the *64-bit* version of the filter packs. I wasn't paying attention the first time I did this and completely screwed up my installation and had to start again from scratch.

Figure 3-31. 64-bit filter packs

Once you've installed the filter pack, you can resume the installation. In my experience it will continue on happily for about 20 minutes, until you hit one last speed bump.

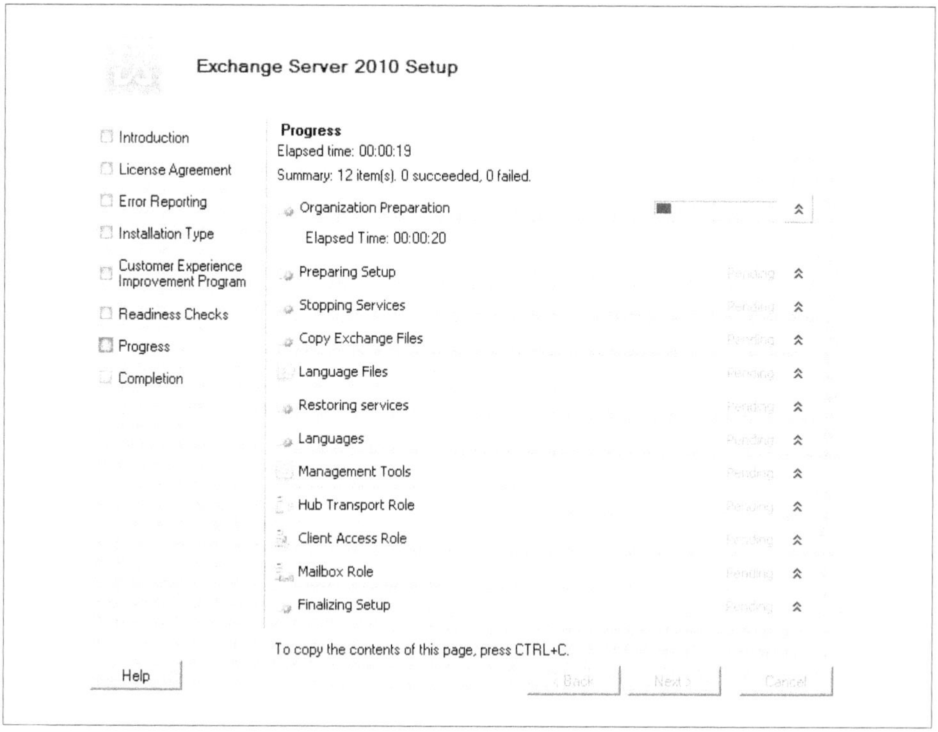

Figure 3-32. Installation progress

Right at the end of the installation process, the installer will yell at you about the Exchange Mailbox Replication Service not having started on time.

Ignore this.

That's right. You read it correctly. *Ignore this warning.* It's meaningless to you. All it really says is that a particular service didn't start in the expected time. If you've built your instance on the Amazon m1.small instance type, then things will take longer to start because there won't be the RAM or CPU horsepower available that Exchange expects.

No need to worry about this. Once you reboot the instance, everything will start up just fine.

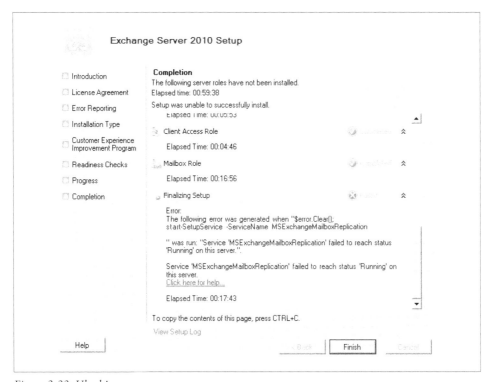

Figure 3-33. Uh oh!

Configuring Your New Mail Beast for Incoming Messages

Once you reboot your instance and all the services start back up, it's time to make some important configuration changes to the server so that it will handle email correctly.

The first thing you have to do is to change the email domains for which the server will accept incoming email.

When one email server tries to deliver email to another email server, it tells the remote server the address to which it wants to submit the message. If, for example, some mail server on the Internet tried to deliver an email to *joe@pizza.com* to a remote server, that server would need to be configured to accept email for the *pizza.com* email domain. This is known as an *accepted domain*.

By default, your new server will be set up for the wrong accepted domain. To change this, do the following:

1. Open the Exchange Management Console from either your desktop or the Start menu.

2. Expand the configuration tree into Microsoft Exchange → Microsoft Exchange On-Premises → Organization Configuration

3. Select Hub Transport as in the screenshot below.

Figure 3-34. New accepted domain

4. Select the Accepted Domains tab.

   You should notice that the domain already configured is something like *yourdomain.local*. That is not what you want. You want to configure your server to accept email destined for *yourdomain.com*. So ...

5. Click the New Accepted Domain link on the right and fill in the pop-up box as follows. (Making sure, of course, to use *your* domain instead of mine!

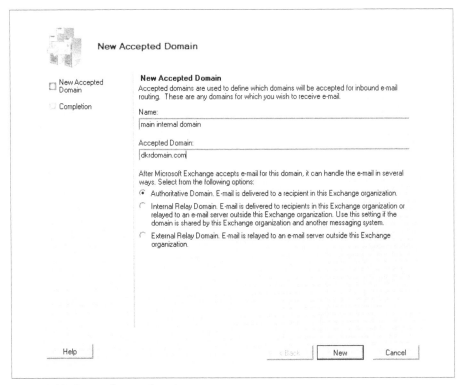

Figure 3-35. Setting the new domain

6. Once you add your new accepted domain, right-click it and set it to default.

7. Finally, right-click the old domain and remove it.

Configuring Outgoing Mail

At this point you are about halfway to a correctly configured server. You've successfully configured your server to accept the correct kind of email addresses. Now it's time to configure it to be able to correctly send mail outbound to the rest of the world.

The component that talks to the outside world is called a *send connector*. By default, your Exchange installation will not be configured with a send connector. That's easily remedied, though. While still in the Hub Transport configuration section, click the Send Connectors tab.

Next, click the New Send Connector link on the right.

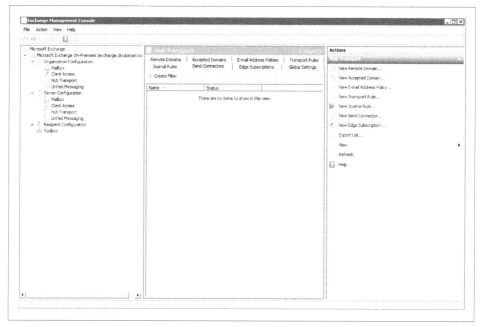

Figure 3-36. Adding a send connector

Give the new connector a name and make certain that the intended use selector for the connector is set to Internet.

Then click Next and Add on the following screen.

In the address space box, enter an asterisk (*). This tells the server that *all* outgoing SMTP mail will be handled through this connector.

On the next screen select the first option: "Use domain name system (DNS) "MX" records to route mail automatically."

Finally, click Next twice and finally New and then Finish.

If all goes well, you'll have a new send connector configured!

There's still one more bit of housekeeping to do, though. Right-click on your new connector and select Properties. In the box titled "Specify the FQDN this connector will provide in response to HELO or EHLO:" enter the name of the external hostname you want to use for this server. For example, since my domain is *dkrdomain.com,* I chose the hostname *mail.dkrdomain.com.*

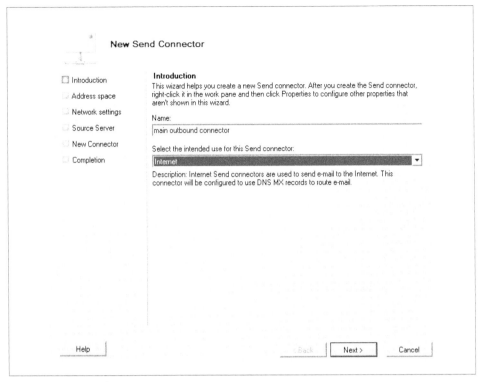

Figure 3-37. Name the connector

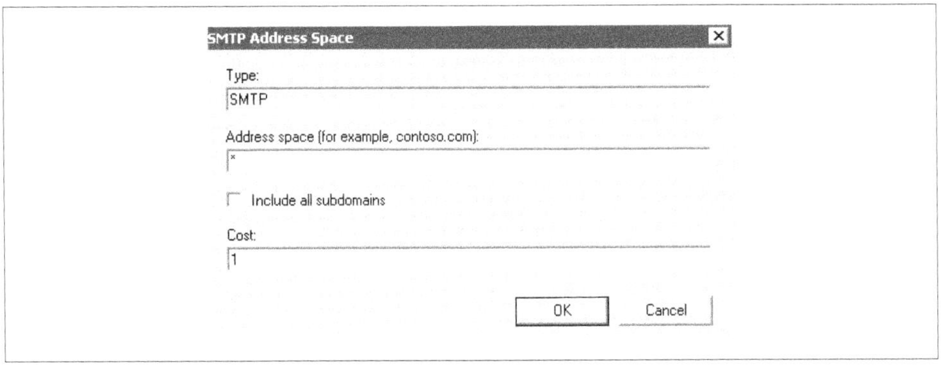

Figure 3-38. SMTP outbound rule

Telling the Outside World About Yourself

Let's review what you've accomplished so far:

1. Create your instance: *check!*
2. Install Exchange Server: *check!*
3. Configure inbound mail routing: *check!*
4. Configure outbound routing: *check!*

So that's it, right?

Er, um ... not quite.

You have two more things to do before we can put this topic to bed.

1. Configure your firewall for inbound mail and Web services
2. Tell the rest of the world which machine will accept email on your behalf

Revisiting Your Security Rules and Firewall

Remember in the beginning of this chapter that you created a new VPC security rule called Exchange that you left empty? Well, now it's time to configure it.

You need to enable two incoming services in order for your Exchange Server to work correctly:

SMTP (TCP port 25)
> The Simple Mail Transfer Protocol (SMTP) is how email servers send email back and forth. It's always on port 25. So you need to add an incoming TCP rule for port 25 in your Exchange security group.

HTTPS (TCP port 443)
> SSL over HTTP (HTTPS) usually runs on TCP port 443. Enabling this traffic into your server will let you use the Outlook Web interface to get mail from any browser and will let your mobile phones sync to your exchange server.

With that in mind, edit the Exchange security group you created earlier to allow these two ports.

Figure 3-39. New rules

Getting the Rest of the World to Send You Mail

The last thing you need to do to get things working is to tell the world that this new server will handle all the email for your domain. For this you need to look up the Elastic IP you created and assigned to this instance in the beginning of this chapter. You can find that information by selecting the instance and looking at the details for the Elastic IP address.

Let's say for the sake of this example that this server is exposed to the world as 107.21.48.16.

You now need to add two new records to the Route 53 record you created in Chapter 1 for your domain.

1. Go to the Route 53 page from the AWS Console.
2. Double-click your domain (in my case, *dkrdomain.com*).
3. Click Create Record Set at the top of the screen, and a new window will open to the right.
4. In the Name box, put in the name `mail`.
5. Set the Type to A - IPv4 Address.
6. In the value box, enter your Elastic IP (in my case, 107.21.48.16).
7. Click Create Record Set at the bottom of the window.

An Internet A record like the one you just set up resolves a regular hostname (in my case *mail.dkrdomain.com*) to a specific IP address (107.21.48.16 in this case). This is just like what you did for your VPN server previously and allows other computers to resolve the host *mail.dkdomain.com* to its IP address.

Next, you have to add a special kind of record called an *MX* record. MX stands for *mail exchanger* and, as you may have guessed, is the key record that tells the world to which computer all email traffic should be delivered.

1. Create another record set.
2. Leave the name empty.
3. Change the type to MX.
4. Enter the following in the value box:

   `10 mail.dkrdomain.com`

   Of course you want to enter *your* mail hostname and not *mine*!
5. Click the Create Record Set button.

These changes could take a few hours to propagate around the Internet, but once they do, everyone will know that all email to your domain goes to the host in the MX record and that the host resolves to your Elastic IP address.

Wrapping Up

We've covered a lot of ground in this chapter. At this point your virtual infrastructure will have VPN, directory, and email services. For some of you that will be enough. If that's the case, then I bid you a fond farewell—but I warn you that you're about to miss some of the really, really cool parts of this book.

Seriously ...

In the coming chapters you will go beyond the basics and really see what this whole Amazon Web Services thing can do when you open her wide up. So put your floaties and goggles on, because it's into the deep end of the pool we go!

## CHAPTER 4

Doing Things the Easy Way

So far in this book you have created your new instances and installed the necessary software on them by hand. There's nothing wrong with that, and it's probably the way you'll wind up configuring your virtual machines as you go on. That said, there is another—and potentially easier—way to accomplish the same thing. You can actually import precreated instances of your software straight into your VPC using the Amazon EC2 API Command Line Tools.

Over the last several years, virtual machines have been growing in popularity as a way to quickly create and scale infrastructure resources. In fact, each of the EC2 instances you've been creating in this book is actually a virtual machine hosted in Amazon's cloud. The two most common formats for virtual machines are the virtual machine disk format (VMDK, created by VMWare Corporation (*http://www.VMWare.com*)) and the Virtual Hard Disk (VHD) format, an invention of Microsoft (*http://www.microsoft .com*). Each format has gained a significant following, and there are now many vendors that package preconfigured versions of their software in one or both of these formats.

The advantage of using one of these preconfigured images is that you can directly import them into the Amazon EC2 infrastructure as a fully ready instance. You can even import them into your existing VPC—if you know the magic words, that is! The way to accomplish these feats of IT magic is with the Amazon EC2 API Command Line Tools.

Introducing the EC2 API Command Line Tools

Amazon is a very developer-friendly entity. For just about every service they offer, they also offer some kind of SDK or other developer tool. The AWS services are no exception. For the purpose of automating common AWS functions—like creating VPCs, starting and stopping an EC2 instance, or just about any other thing you can think of—Amazon has provided a wonderful set of command-line tools. The set you care about in this section of the book are those having to do with EC2 instances and VPCs. These collections of functions all exist in one set of command-line tools known as the EC2 API Command Line Tools.

There are too many to list completely here, but they cover approximately these functional areas:

- AMIs/images
- Availability zones and regions
- Customer gateways
- DHCP options
- Elastic block store
- Elastic IP addresses
- Elastic network interfaces
- Instances
- Internet gateways
- Key pairs
- Monitoring
- Network ACLs
- Placement groups
- Reserved instances
- Route tables
- Security groups
- Spot instances
- Subnets
- Tags
- Virtual machine (VM) import and export
- VPCs
- Virtual private gateways
- VPN connections
- Windows

Yikes! That's a lot of stuff!

For your purposes, you're only going to be concerned with three specific functions from the VM import function group.

- `ec2-cancel-conversion-task`
- `ec2-describe-conversion-tasks`
- `ec2-import-instance`

The `ec2-import-instance` command does exactly what it sounds like. It imports a virtual machine you have on a local computer and converts the VM to a valid EC2 instance. This process is called a *conversion task*. It therefore stands to reason that `ec2-describe-conversion-tasks` gets information about your currently running tasks and `ec2-cancel-conversion-task` cancels a task that's in process.

Downloading, Installing, and Configuring the Tools

Before you can use these tools, you need to install them on your local machine.

In this chapter, I'm going to assume that you're installing these tools on a Windows machine. I make this assumption because a) that's the dominant desktop platform in IT and b) it's the trickiest to get working.

The EC2 Command Line tools can be found at the Amazon developer site (*http://s3 .amazonaws.com/ec2-downloads/ec2-api-tools.zip*). They come in a ZIP file, so be sure to unzip them someplace you can easily remember, like `c:\ec2-tools`.

The next thing you need is a current version of a Java runtime environment (JRE), which you can get from the Oracle Java site (*http://java.sun.com*). Once you've downloaded and run the installer for the JRE, you can continue. For this chapter I'm going to use the installation path of my JRE: *c:\Program Files(x86)\java\jre7*.

Creating a Client Certificate

Many of the EC2 command-line tools also require a client certificate to identify you. This is for your protection, I promise. Since you probably don't have such a pair from Amazon yet, let's get those now.

1. Go to the main Amazon developer portal (*https://forums.aws.amazon.com/index .jspa*).
2. Select the pull-down in the upper right titled My Account/Console, and select Security Credentials.
3. You might be prompted to sign in to your Amazon developer account, so do that. If not, just continue.
4. In the Access Credentials part of the page, click the tab marked X.509 Certificates.
5. If this book is your first experience with Amazon AWS, you will need to create a certificate pair. This pair consists of two parts: a *private key file* that you must store locally and a *certificate file* that you can always redownload if you need to.

You will get one—*and only one*—opportunity to save the private-key file associated with your certificate. It will automatically download through your browser when you create a new pair.

Save this file someplace safe and memorable.

I cannot stress this warning enough: if you misplace this file (as I have) you will need to invalidate the certificate it corresponds to and create a new pair.

6. Click the Create a New Certificate link.

7. A new window will pop up with two buttons: one to download the private-key file and one to download the new certificate. Click each button in turn, and save each file someplace safe.

8. Click the Access Keys tab.

9. Copy the Access Key ID to a text file someplace safe and private.

10. Click Show and copy the Secret Access Key value to the same file.

Setting Up Your Environment

With the client certificate out of the way, you need to set some very handy environment variables. On your Windows machine, right-click My Computer and select Properties → Advanced Settings → Environment Variables.

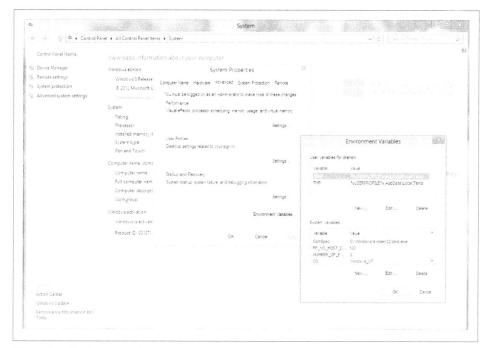

Figure 4-1. The System environment settings

You need to set the following system variables:

EC2_HOME
> The location on disk where you unzipped the EC2 tools. You want the directory that contains the *bin* subdirectory.

JAVA_HOME
> Where the current JRE is installed. In my case that's *c:\Program Files(x86)\Java \Jre7*.

EC2_PRIVATE_KEY
> The full path to the private-key file you downloaded earlier.

EC2_CERT
> The full path to the X.509 certificate you also saved.

ACCESS_KEY_ID
> The value of the Access Key ID you saved earlier.

SECRET_ACCESS_KEY
> The value of the Secret Access Key you saved earlier.

PATH
> This is a preexisting variable that defines where Windows goes to look for software you want to run. You need to append the string %EC2_HOME% to it so it looks something like:

>   c:\Windows System;c:\someplace else;%EC2_HOME%

> If you're running on Mac OS X (as I am) or on Linux, you probably just want to create a simple shell script that exports these variables, or you can define them in a well-known place for whichever shell you use—in my case *.bash-profile*, because my native shell is Bash.

Now that your tools are downloaded and configured, it's time to have some fun!

Downloading and Importing a Test Image

Since the point of this chapter is to teach you how to upload your own VMs as instances in your VPC, you should first start with a test image.

> Although the EC2 service supports both Linux and Windows Server instances, at the time of this writing you can import only images built on Windows Server 2008, 2008 R1, and 2008 R2 through the command-line tools. It's a bummer, I know, but I'm sure Amazon will get around to rectifying it in the near future. They tend to be pretty good at that stuff.

Not all of you will already have a handy VHD or VMDK to test with; if you don't, you can go get one from our friends at Microsoft:

1. Go to the Microsoft Exchange Server Software Evaluation Page (*http://www.micro soft.com/en-us/download/details.aspx?id=5002*).

2. You may need to sign in with a valid Microsoft Live account. Get one if you don't have one.

3. Download all the files from the page.

Figure 4-2. Files to download

4. Run the executable once all the files are downloaded.

   The VHD image is actually wrapped in a self-extracting RAR archive.

If you're doing this on a Mac, don't worry that one of the files is a Windows executable. Just grab a copy of the free version of the Stuffit Expander (*http://www.stuffit.com/mac-expander-download .html*) utility and select the *.exe* file. It will expand just fine from there. Alternatively, there's always the great open source Rar Expander (*http://rarexpander.sourceforge.net/Downloads.html*).

My machine extracted the VHD to *ExchangeDemos\SLC-DC01\VirtualHard Disks*.

5. Change directory into the extraction directory.

The command you're interested in is `ec2-import-instance`. A shortened version of its syntax is:

```
ec2-import-instance -t instance_type [-g group]
                    -f file_format -a architecture -b s3_bucket_name [-o owner]
                    -w secret_key [-s volume_size ][-z availability_zone]
                              [-d description]
                              [--user-data-file disk_image_filename]
                              [--subnet subnet_id]
```

Table 4-1. ec2-import-instance options

Option Name	Description	Required
`-t, --instance-type` `instance_type`	Specifies the type of instance to be launched.	Yes
	Type: String	
	Default: `m1.small`	
	Valid values: `m1.small` | `m1.large` | `m1.xlarge` | `c1.medium` | `c1.xlarge` | `m2.xlarge` | `m2.2xlarge` | `m2.4xlarge`	
	Example: `-t m1.small`	
`-g, --group` *group*	The security group within which the instances should be run. Determines the ingress firewall rules that are applied to the launched instances. Only one security group is supported for an instance.	No
	Type: String	
	Default: Your default security group	
	Example: `-g myGroup`	
`-f, --format` *file_format*	The file format of the disk image.	Yes
	Type: String	
	Default: None	
	Values: `VMDK` | `RAW` | `VHD`	
	Example: `-f VMDK`	
`-a, --architecture` *architecture*	The architecture of the image.	Yes

Option Name	Description	Required
	Type: String	
	Default: i386	
	Values: i386 | x86_64	
	Condition: Required if instance type is specified; otherwise defaults to i386.	
	Example: -a i386	
--bucket *s3_bucket_name*	The Amazon S3 destination bucket for the manifest.	Yes
	Type: String	
	Default: None	
	Condition: The --manifest-url parameter is not specified.	
	Example: myawsbucket	
-o, --owner-akid *access_key_id*	Access key ID of the bucket owner.	No
	Type: String	
	Default: None	
	Example: AKIAIOSFODNN7EXAMPLE	
-w, --owner-sak *secret_access_key*	Secret access key of the bucket owner.	Yes
	Type: String	
	Default: None	
	Example: wJalrXUtnFEMI/K7MDENG/bPxRfiCYEXAMPLE KEY	
--prefix *prefix*	Prefix for the manifest file and disk image file parts within the Amazon S3 bucket.	No
	Type: String	
	Default: None	
	Example: --prefix MyDiskParts	
--manifest-url *url*	The URL for an existing import manifest file already uploaded to Amazon S3.	No
	Type: String	
	Default: None. This option cannot be specified if the --bucket option is present.	
	Example: my-ami.manifest.xml	
-s, --volume-size *volume_size*	The size of the Amazon Elastic Block Store volume, in Gibibytes (2^{30} bytes), that will hold the converted image. If not specified, EC2 calculates the value using the disk image file.	No
	Type: String	

Option Name	Description	Required
	Default: None	
	Example: -s 30	
-z, --availability-zone *availability_zone*	The Availability Zone for the converted VM.	No
	Type: String	
	Default: None	
	Values: Use ec2-describe-availability-zones for a list of values	
	Example: -z us-east-1	
-d, --description *description*	An optional, free-form comment returned verbatim during subsequent calls to ec2-describe-conversion-tasks.	No
	Type: String	
	Default: None	
	Constraint: Maximum length of 255 characters	
	Example: -d Test of ec2-import-instance	
--user-data *user_data*	User data to be made available to the imported instance.	No
	Type: String	
	Default: None	
	Example: --user-data This is user data	
--user-data-file *disk_image_filename*	The file containing user data made available to the imported instance.	No
	Type: String	
	Default: None	
	Example: --user-data-file my_data_file	
--subnet *subnet_id*	If you're using Amazon Virtual Private Cloud, this specifies the ID of the subnet into which you're launching the instance.	No
	Type: String	
	Default: None	
	Example: --subnet subnet-f3e6ab83	
--private-ip-address *ip_address*	If you're using Amazon Virtual Private Cloud, this specifies the specific IP address within subnet to use.	No
	Type: String	
	Default: None	
	Example: --private-ip-address 10.0.0.3	
--monitor	Enables monitoring of the specified instance(s).	No
	Type: String	

Option Name	Description	Required
	Default: None	
	Example: `--monitor`	
`--instance-initiated-shutdown-behavior` *behavior*	If an instance shutdown is initiated, this determines whether the instance stops or terminates.	No
	Type: String	
	Default: None	
	Values: `stop	terminate`	
	Example: `--instance-initiated-shutdown-behavior stop`	
`-x, --expires` *days*	Validity period for the signed Amazon S3 URLS that allow EC2 to access the manifest.	No
	Type: String	
	Default: 30 days	
	Example: `-x 10`	
`--ignore-region-affinity`	Ignore the verification check to determine that the bucket's Amazon S3 Region matches the EC2 Region where the conversion task is created.	No
	Type: None	
	Default: None	
	Example: `--ignore-region-affinity`	
`--dry-run`	Does not create an import task, only validates that the disk image matches a known type.	No
	Type: None	
	Default: None	
	Example: `--dry-run`	
`--no-upload`	Does not upload a disk image to Amazon S3, only creates an import task. To complete the import task and upload the disk image, use `ec2-resume-import`.	No
	Type: None	
	Default: None	
	Example: `--no-upload`	
`--dont-verify-format`	Does not verify the file format. You don't recommend this option because it can result in a failed conversion.	No
	Type: None	
	Default: None	
	Example: `--dont-verify-format`	

You don't need all of these options, of course. Since you want to launch your new instance inside of your existing VPC, your command will take the form of:

```
ec2-import-instance -o %ACCESS_KEY_ID% -w %SECRET_ACCESS_KEY% -f VHD -a
            x86_64 --bucket S3_bucket_name -z zone_of_VPC --subnet
            subnet_ID_for_VPC path_to_VHD_or_VMDK
```

In my particular case, my VPC is in availability zone us-east-1a and my subnet ID is subnet-8aafcce2. I also created an S3 bucket named dkr_imports as temporary storage for my import jobs. With all this in mind, my command will be:

```
ec2-import-instance -o %ACCESS_KEY_ID% -w %SECRET_ACCESS_KEY% -f VHD -a
            x86_64 --bucket dkr_imports -z us-east-1a --subnet subnet-8aafcce2
            SLC-DC01.vhd
```

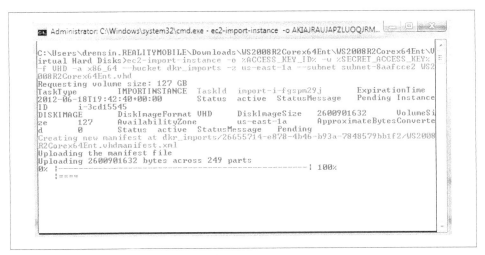

Figure 4-3. A successfully running import job

 You need a valid S3 bucket for this process because that's where Amazon stores your uploaded instance while it converts it to a VPC. No worries if you don't already have one created. As long as you specify a name, the command will create a bucket with that name for you.

If the image upload process went well, you should receive a message like:

```
Done.
Average speed was 4.852 MBps.
The disk image for import-i-fgspm29j has been uploaded to Amazon S3 where it is being
converted into an EC2 instance.
You may monitor the progress of this task by running ec2-describe-conversion-tasks.
When the task is completed, you may use ec2-delete-disk-image to remove the image from
S3.
```

The parts highlighted in bold are the important bits of this message. First, it has given you the name of the import task: import-i-fgspm29j. Second, it has told you that you can check on the status of your import by running `ec2-describe-conversion-tasks`; finally, it conveys that you can delete your intermediate file from your S3 bucket using the `ec2-delete-disk-image` command.

As you may have inferred from these messages, the import process is actually three separate processes:

Upload

> This is the step you just completed where your VHD was uploaded to Amazon for conversion into a runnable instance in your VPC.

Image conversion

> Once the image is uploaded, Amazon needs to convert the image to an intermediate format it uses to populate an EBS volume that it will attach to your new instance.

Instance creation

> The final stage of the process is where Amazon creates an instance and attaches the new EBS volume to it as its root storage device.

If you run `ec2-describe-conversion-tasks` on task `import-i-fgspm29j`, you might see something like:

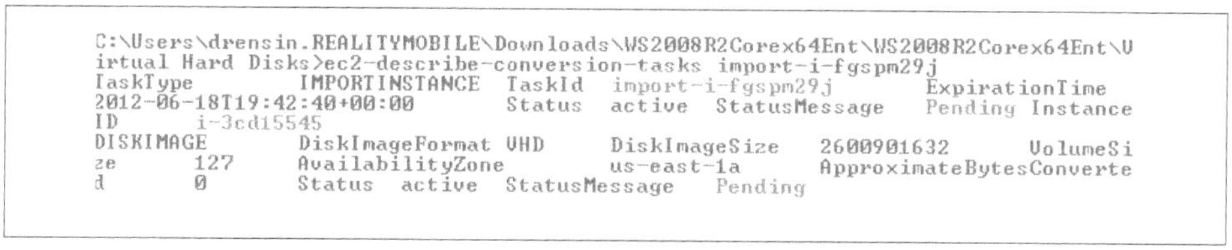

```
C:\Users\drensin.REALITYMOBILE\Downloads\WS2008R2Corex64Ent\WS2008R2Corex64Ent\V
irtual Hard Disks>ec2-describe-conversion-tasks import-i-fgspm29j
TaskType        IMPORTINSTANCE  TaskId   import-i-fgspm29j         ExpirationTime
2012-06-18T19:42:40+00:00           Status   active  StatusMessage   Pending Instance
ID     i-3cd15545
DISKIMAGE       DiskImageFormat UHD      DiskImageSize   2600901632       VolumeSi
ze      127     AvailabilityZone         us-east-1a      ApproximateBytesConverte
d       0       Status   active  StatusMessage   Pending
```

Figure 4-4. Status check 1

I've highlighted some important parts. The first thing to notice is that you're getting two statuses with this command. The higher one in the output is the instance creation status, while the lower one is the conversion status. Since I ran this command immediately after the upload, you can see that both tasks are still pending.

If I wait a little while and run the command again, I get the following:

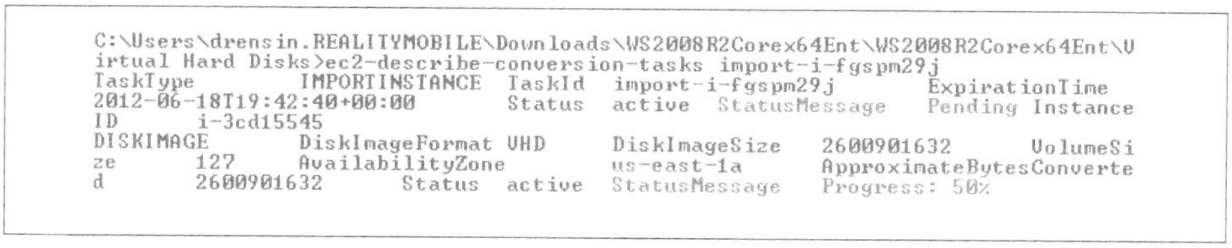

```
C:\Users\drensin.REALITYMOBILE\Downloads\WS2008R2Corex64Ent\WS2008R2Corex64Ent\V
irtual Hard Disks>ec2-describe-conversion-tasks import-i-fgspm29j
TaskType        IMPORTINSTANCE  TaskId   import-i-fgspm29j         ExpirationTime
2012-06-18T19:42:40+00:00           Status   active  StatusMessage   Pending Instance
ID     i-3cd15545
DISKIMAGE       DiskImageFormat UHD      DiskImageSize   2600901632       VolumeSi
ze      127     AvailabilityZone         us-east-1a      ApproximateBytesConverte
d       2600901632      Status   active  StatusMessage   Progress: 50%
```

Figure 4-5. Status check 2: 5 minutes later

Notice here that the creation status is still pending while the conversion status is at 50 percent.

Next, I wait 30 more minutes and get the following:

```
C:\Users\drensin.REALITYMOBILE\Downloads\WS2008R2Corex64Ent\WS2008R2Corex64Ent\V
irtual Hard Disks>ec2-describe-conversion-tasks import-i-fgspm29j
TaskType       IMPORTINSTANCE  TaskId  import-i-fgspm29j        ExpirationTime
2012-06-18T19:42:40+00:00       Status  active  StatusMessage   Progress: 19%
InstanceID      i-3cd15545
DISKIMAGE       DiskImageFormat UHD     DiskImageSize   2600901632      VolumeId
        vol-132bb77d    VolumeSize      127     AvailabilityZone        us-east-
1a      ApproximateBytesConverted       2600901632      Status  completed
```

Figure 4-6. Status check 3: 30 minutes later

The instance creation process is at 19 percent and conversion process is marked as completed.

In general, expect to wait *at least* an hour after your upload for the instance to be created and online.

For those of you running on either Linux or Mac OS X, you can check on the status of your import every 5 minutes by running this handy command:

```
while true;
  do ec2dct import-i-fgspm29j | grep StatusMessage | cut -f 7-10; sleep 300; clear;
done
```

Of course you need to substitute your import task ID for mine, but you get the point.

Eventually, the process will complete and you will be able to start your new instance from the EC2 instance list in the AWS Management Console.

This instance we've uploaded happens to be an entire IT infrastructure on one machine: domain controller, Active Directory, and Exchange server. If you really wanted to get up and running fast, you could just import this instance into a regular EC2 instance and call it a day, but you want more service than this provides. (And doing so would make this book wicked short!)

Please note that when this instance starts you will be able to RDP in to it from your gateway machine, but we'll need special credentials to get in. More on that in a minute.

While you're waiting for your import to finish, you should go over some do's and dont's as they relate to importing an instance into AWS.

Amazon has a very detailed guide on how to prepare your existing VMs (*http://docs .amazonwebservices.com/AWSEC2/latest/UserGuide/UploadingYourInstancesandVo lumes.html*) (Citrix, VMWare, and Microsoft Hyper-V). Read it twice. It will shortcut lots of potential problems. In the meantime, here are some highlights:

Ensure that remote desktop is enabled.

If RDP is not already enabled on the image you are importing, you will have no way to connect to it once it's an EC2 instance.

Windows firewall must allow public RDP traffic.

There's no point enabling RDP if the firewall won't allow public IP addresses to use it.

Autologon must be disabled.

You can't RDP into a Windows Server machine if autologon is enabled, because there's no username/password prompting.

No Windows updates should be pending.

When AWS first boots the new instance, the very last thing you want to happen is for it to start into an update cycle.

 While you're waiting for your import and conversion task to complete, I'd like to specifically thank Peter Beckman from the EC2 Import/Export team at Amazon Web Services. My first couple of attempts to do this failed for some subtle reasons, and he was super helpful while I was troubleshooting. If you get a chance, drop him a shout-out at his email address (*mailto:pbeck@amazon.com*) and tell him "thanks" for helping your humble author!

If everything goes according to plan, you should see this:

```
TaskType        IMPORTINSTANCE  TaskId  import-i-ffsicbou     ExpirationTime 2
012-06-21T16:34:15+00:00        Status  completed    InstanceID    i-a632ab
df
DISKIMAGE       DiskImageFormat VHD      DiskImageSize  22329183232    VolumeIv
ol-1b9ff075     VolumeSize      127      AvailabilityZone      us-east-1a    A
pproximateBytesConverted        22329183232     Status  completed
```

Figure 4-7. All systems go!

When you go back to your AWS console and look at your EC2 instances, you should see one like this:

Figure 4-8. Ready to start

The instance has no label because you didn't give it one during the import. You could have, but you already had a bunch of command-line options to manage. Go ahead and click the field and give it a meaningful name—maybe something like **The Instance I'm Going to Delete in 2 Minutes**. Then, right-click and start it up.

Now you should verify that everything is working OK.

1. Find the internal IP address of the instance from its details page. In my case it's 10.0.0.31.

2. Connect to the gateway via your VPN.

3. Using your RDP client, connect to the gateway machine you created.

4. Once there, open a command prompt and type **ping 10.0.0.31**. Of course, substitute your IP address. If you get the following, things are looking up.

```
C:\Users\Administrator>ping 10.0.0.31

Pinging 10.0.0.31 with 32 bytes of data:
Reply from 10.0.0.31: bytes=32 time=7ms TTL=128
Reply from 10.0.0.31: bytes=32 time<1ms TTL=128
Reply from 10.0.0.31: bytes=32 time<1ms TTL=128
Reply from 10.0.0.31: bytes=32 time=43ms TTL=128

Ping statistics for 10.0.0.31:
    Packets: Sent = 4, Received = 4, Lost = 0 (0% loss),
Approximate round trip times in milli-seconds:
    Minimum = 0ms, Maximum = 43ms, Average = 12ms
```

5. Now for the big test. RDP to the new instance by typing the command

```
mstsc /v:10.0.0.31 /console /admin
```

Again, use your IP address.

 This particular image from Microsoft is already its own domain. You will need the following credentials to log in to it:

- Username: **contoso\Administrator**
- Password: **pass@word1**

6. Accept the certificate if asked.

If all goes well, you will have successfully connected to your newly imported instance. Congratulations!

Go ahead and poke around the instance for a bit if you like, but eventually you're going to have to terminate it. You don't need it and it's not a good idea to have two different domains and controllers on the same subnet.

Cleaning Up and Wrapping Up

Once we've had your fun with your new instance, it's time to clean up. You need to do two things:

1. Clean up the temporary import files created for you in S3.

2. Terminate the instance.

The first is accomplished with the following command:

```
ec2-delete-disk-image -t import-i-ffsicbou -o %ACCESS_KEY_ID% -w %SECRET_ACCESS_KEY%
```

```
0% |------------------------------------------------| 100%
   |================================================|
```

Done

This command deletes all temporary files associated with the import task specified after the -t flag.

The final thing to do is to terminate the instance by right-clicking it in the AWS console and selecting Terminate.

So ... what have you learned?

If you already have Windows Server-based virtual machines running in your existing infrastructure, you can easily and securely import them into the AWS cloud. This is very handy when migrating from a traditional on-site infrastructure to a cloud-based architecture.

As it happens, you can also do this process in reverse. You can create and configure an instance in the AWS cloud and then export it to VM to use on a physical machine—maybe a demo laptop, for example.

Of course, we've only scratched the surface of what the EC2 command-line tools can do. You can also, for instance, upload a raw disk image and attach it to an already configured instance as another disk drive—and that's just the beginning. But this is a book about IT virtualization, not scripting or programming, and that subject alone could go a solid hundred pages.

## CHAPTER 5

Do You Have Some Time to Chat?

If you're reading this in electronic form you probably haven't noticed that you're about halfway through the book. Now is a pretty convenient time to take stock and talk a little about what's next.

By now you have the following IT elements running:

- Your own private cloud using a VPC
- Your own DNS management system using Route 53
- A secure means of connecting to your VPC, courtesy of OpenVPN
- A functioning and properly configured Windows domain
- Working enterprise email using Microsoft Exchange

Those are things that any real infrastructure *must* have.

This next half of the book is about the things you might *like* to have. They include:

- Enterprise chat services
- IP telephony
- Automated management and health services

When all of these things are configured and running, you'll be the envy of all the neighbors!

So let's start at the top of list and set up an enterprise-class chat service.

Chat? Really? Isn't That So 1990s?

Like bell bottoms and boy bands, chat services are making a comeback.

Skeptical?

Take a look at any person under the age of 30 and how they use their cell phone. Sure, sometimes they're talking on it, but most of the time they're texting back and forth with friends and family. Sometime in the middle of 2011 the amount of time the average person spent on a cell phone using data services like texting actually surpassed the amount of time they spent using the phone for its principle function—voice communications.

Need more proof that chat is the new voice?

Hugely popular Web services like Twitter and Facebook much more closely resemble group chat services than they do email or voice.

In fact, almost any place you look you'll find chat.

Online gaming has a huge chat component to it now, as does just about any product support page you visit on the Internet.

I have actually seen people sitting in the same room using their laptops to chat with each other!

It's like some Philip K. Dick (*http://en.wikipedia.org/wiki/Phillip_K_Dick*) dystopian future where we all take a vow of silence but feel compelled to talk more than ever. So we chat.

One Standard to Rule Them All

In the early 2000s there was a major war over which standard would rule them all in the realm of chat services.

In one corner there were the proprietary protocols like AOL's AIM and Microsoft's MSN. In the other corner there were the open standards, Jabber being the most popular.

In the end, everyone decided that the world would be a much nicer place if we took to heart the admonition of Rodney King (*http://www.usatoday.com/news/top25-quotes .htm*) and agreed that yes, we all *can* just get along. Jabber won and eventually morphed into the global messaging standard named *XMPP*.

XMPP stands for the Extensible Messaging and Presence Protocol and is the IETF's formalization of the base XML streaming protocols for instant messaging and presence, developed within the Jabber community starting in 1999. When XMPP was submitted to the IETF in 2000 to become an Internet standard, the name was changed from Jabber so as to avoid any confusion with the commercial instant messaging service by the same name.

Jabber (the company) was eventually acquired by Cisco.

You can read all about the history of XMPP at the XMMP.org (*http:// www.xmpp.org*) website.

Step 1: Picking an XMPP Server

There are literally dozens of XMPP servers available in the marketplace right now. Many are free, some are commercial, and every major operating system is well represented. You can find a pretty comprehensive list of them at the XMPP.org (*http://www.xmpp .org*) website.

So how do you pick?

Here are my criteria. Yours may differ.

Must run on Windows Server 2008
> Every new EC2 instance you create will cost a little more money each month, so it behooves you to double up where you can. The VPN, PDC, and AD services all run on one box, so I'm going to install the XMPP server on the same instance as the Exchange server. (Think of it as the communications instance in the VPC.)

Should support the widest possible array of XMPP protocol extensions
> Since the adoption of the core XMPP standard, a number of very handy extensions have also been adopted. They are known as *XEPs*, or XMPP Extension Protocols. For example, they define ways for an XMPP server to use an enterprise directory service like LDAP or Active Directory to authenticate users, ways of transforming XMPP messages to and from standard email, and just about any other thing you could want your XMPP server to do.

> To enable the greatest number of features going forward, I'm going to look for a server that enables the greatest number of these extensions and has an active development community that will ensure that new extensions are adopted, as well.

Must be free or darn close to it
> I'm cheap. You might as well be, too.

Several good candidates fit these criteria. As it happens, I have a fair amount of experience with all of them and, by far, my personal preference is a server named Openfire (*http://www.igniterealtime.org/projects/openfire/index.jsp*). I like it because it's been in active development for several years, supports nearly all the currently published XEPs, has both a free and commercial version, and runs nicely on Windows Server 2008.

You can, of course, pick any server you like, but I'll be focusing on installing and configuring OpenFire for use in the VPC.

Step 2: Downloading and Installing

Here's the quick and easy way to get up and going.

1. VPN into the VPC.
2. RDP to the gateway machine.
3. RDP from the gateway machine to the exchange machine.

4. On the Exchange instance, go to Start → Control Panel → Internet Options → Security.

5. Select Trusted Sites.

6. Click the Sites button and add *.igniterealtime.org to the list of trusted sites. This step adds any site in the igniterealtime.org domain to the trusted sites list, and will let you download Openfire and run the installer without a lot of hassle from Internet Explorer.

7. Open Internet Explorer and go to the download page for Openfire (http://www .igniterealtime.org/projects/openfire/index.jsp).

8. Click the ▧▧▧▧▧ button.

9. Choose the Windows platform under the Openfire section and select the link that ends in .exe.

At this point the installer should download and run. Accept all the defaults, agree to all the conditions, and after you click Finish, you should be greeted with the following window.

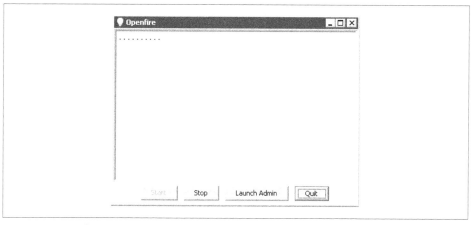

Figure 5-1. Openfire

Go ahead and click Launch Admin and your browser will open to the Openfire setup wizard.

Configuration

Installing the server is one thing, but now you need to configure it. I'm not going to walk you through the default configuration because a) that's boring and b) if you follow this chapter exactly you'll have a server that's truly integrated into your enterprise infrastructure (which is *not* boring!).

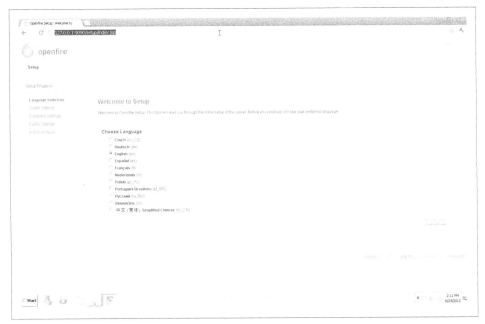

Figure 5-2. *The Openfire setup wizard*

Select your language and click Continue.

The next screen you come to should be for the server settings.

 In the field named Domain, be sure to put in the external name of your Exchange server. Mine is called *exchange.dkrdomain.com*, so that's the value I'm going to use. If you named yours something like *mail.mydomain.com* back in Chapter 3, use that.

If you don't do exactly this, life will be very ugly for you a little later when you start to configure XMPP clients to talk to your server!

On the next screen, select Embedded Database, since you don't have an enterprise database management systems (DBMS) set up in the VPC.

Now comes my favorite part of the installation!

On the Profile Settings page, select the option Directory Server (LDAP). I'm going to show you how to configure Openfire to talk to your Active Directory and use those services to authenticate your chat users. That way you won't have to maintain two separate user lists.

Click Continue.

LDAP Fields

LDAP (*Lightweight Directory Access Protocol*) is the standard way software inquires about the directory information for an organization. In your case that will be your users and groups. Some important LDAP fields are:

Distinguished Name (DN)
> The name that uniquely identifies an entry in the directory.

Domain Component (DC)
> Each component of the domain. For example, *google.com* would be written as DC=google,DC=com.

Organizational Unit (OU)
> The organizational unit (or sometimes the user group) that the user is part of. If the user is part of more than one group, you may specify that; for example, OU=Lawyer,OU=Judge.

Common Name (CN)
> The individual object (person's name, meeting room, recipe name, job title, etc.) for whom/which you are querying.

For example, in my VPC I am *drensin* in the domain of *dkrdomain.local*. Therefore my LDAP DN would be CN=drensin,DC=dkrdomain,DC=local.

You should now be on a page titled Profile Settings: Connection Settings.

Figure 5-3. Profile settings

This is the first of two pages where you will configure your XMPP server to use your Active Directory to manage users, groups, and passwords.

Let's take it one item at a time.

Server Type

Select Active Directory.

Host

Put in the IP address or *internal* name of your gateway machine. Mine is 10.0.0.209.

Port

The default LDAP port for an AD server is 389, so you can leave this value alone.

Base DN

This is the root DN from which all users and groups will be polled. Because my internal domain is *dkrdomain.local*, my value for this field is `dc=dkrdo main,dc=local`. Be certain to use *your* internal AD domain for this value.

Administrator DN

Openfire will need a valid username and password on your domain to query the AD server. In my case I'm going to give it my domain administrator account. In a basic AD configuration, all users exist in a group called *Users*. The Administrator user for my domain would therefore be `cn=Administrator,cn=Users,dc=dkrdo main,dc=local`.

Password

The password for the account you just entered.

 The configuration you've set up in this book does not divide your users or groups into separate OUs, so the configuration for Openfire isn't terribly complicated. If, down the road, you wind up federating your users or groups into different OUs, you may have to change things in the Openfire configuration.

 Caveat Googler! If you Google for instructions on how to set up Openfire in a Windows domain, be certain the instructions are for a Windows Server 2008 domain. The instructions for earlier versions of Windows Server are different and will frustrate the heck out of you. I know this from personal and painful firsthand experience!

Feeling lucky? Good.

Click the Test Settings button to test that Openfire can use your Administrator (or whichever account you chose) account to connect to your AD server. If the test succeeds, go ahead and move on to the next screen. If not, check your settings carefully to be sure you've followed my instructions.

This next screen, User Mapping, will test that you entered the correct base DN information on the previous screen. You shouldn't have to modify a thing on this screen. Just click the Test Settings button at the bottom.

Once again, if you were careful to put in the right information in the correct format on the previous screen, you should see a window pop up with basic account information for one of the users in your domain.

 Don't worry that the address, phone number, and other similar items are blank. You probably didn't fill them in when you created your users. I've tested this pretty extensively, and the default field mappings that Openfire provide are correct.

When you're satisfied, move on to the next page, Group Mappings.

You can test the settings here as you did on the previous two screens, but if you've been successful thus far, there's really no need to.

The final screen asks you for the name of a domain user to use as the administrative account for Openfire. For the sake of consistency, I used my Administrator account. If you don't want to use that account for some reason, just pick another user in your domain. Once you add this user, be sure to test its credentials by clicking the ⚑ icon next to its name.

Go ahead and finish the wizard.

Configuring the Network

Congratulations, you have a working XMPP server ... that you have no way of reaching from the Internet.

In this section you will learn how to configure your VPC, and the instance on which you installed Openfire, to accept two kinds of traffic from the outside world:

* Secure XMPP traffic on port 5223
* HTTPS traffic for the Openfire main administration screen on port 9091

Windows Has a Firewall?

Up until this point in the book you've have been installing conventional Microsoft products in your VPC. These products use ports and require firewall rules that automatically get set up when the products install. For example, when you activated Active Directory on your VPN instance, Windows Server automatically added a rule to the firewall running on the instance to allow traffic on port 389, the default LDAP port.

Yes, you read that right. I didn't say anything about the firewall guarding your VPC. I said the *Windows Firewall*.

Every Windows instance in your VPC comes configured with a built-in firewall. Most times you won't notice it because it comes preconfigured to handle most use cases.

Other times the software you install will make the necessary changes to the firewall rules on your behalf.

In the case of your XMPP server, however, neither of these things happened. You will have to configure both the built-in Windows firewall *and* the security group associated with your instance in order to get secure XMPP traffic to and from the Internet.

By default (and convention), secure XMPP using SSL runs over the standard port 5223. (Insecure traffic runs over port 5222, but you're not going to allow that.) In addition, Openfire allows you to connect to its administrative Web interface over SSL on port 9091. These are the two ports you need to open.

The first step is to configure the Windows Firewall settings on the Windows instance running Openfire.

Select Start → Control Panel → Windows Firewall and you should see the following:

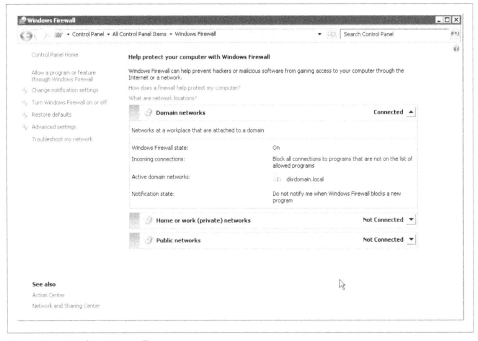

Figure 5-4. Windows Firewall

Click the "Advanced settings" link on the left.

 Don't get ahead of yourself and accidentally click the "Allow a program or feature through Windows Firewall" link. That won't get you where you need to be. You need the advanced settings.

On the screen that appears, click the Inbound Rules item on the left and then the New Rule link on the right.

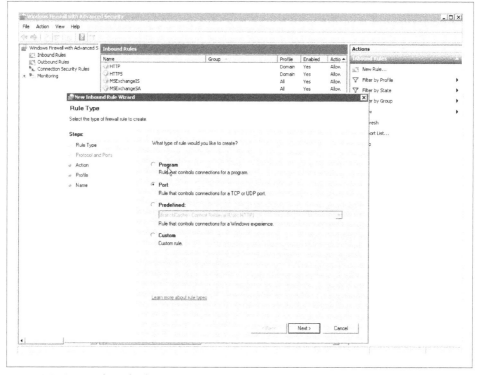

Figure 5-5. A new inbound rule

In this case you don't want to allow access to a specific program through the firewall. You want to allow two ports associated with a new service you've installed.

Change the default selection from Program to Port, and click Next.

The XMPP protocol (like the HTTPS protocol) is TCP-based rather than UDP-based, so you can leave the first setting as is.

Make sure "Specific local ports" is selected and type in the values **5223,9091**. Then click Next.

Click Next again to allow the connection to come from any of the security domains the firewall defines, and Next once more to give your rule a name you can remember—I used XMPP Traffic. Finally, click Finish.

You can close all the Windows Firewall windows now.

Enabling the VPC

Telling the Windows Firewall about your new ports is only the first of the two necessary steps. Now you need to tell your VPC that it's OK to let that inbound traffic through.

Open your web browser to the Amazon Web Services Management Console and navigate to the VPC tab.

Select Security Groups on the left, and highlight the security group you created in "Setting Up the Instance" on page 41 specifically for your Exchange server.

Add two new inbound TCP rules: one for port 5223 and another for port 9091.

 Windows Firewall was kind enough to accept ports delimited by commas; in your case 5223, 9091. Amazon VPC security groups, however, will not. So if your ports are nonconsecutive (as they are in this case), you need to add a rule for each port.

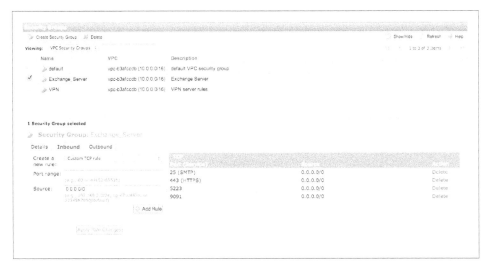

Figure 5-6. Adding the inbound rules

Apply the changes and you're done!

Well ...

Almost done ...

You still need to test things.

Installing and Configuring Your XMPP Client

Like a new car, the best way to test your new XMPP server is to take it for a quick spin around the block. That means installing and configuring an XMPP client on your desktop and actually sending and receiving messages.

In this section I'll quickly walk you through just that.

 Even if you're a devout Windows user, please read the section on setting up the Mac client. It contains some information you will find handy when setting up your Windows XMPP client.

Mac OS X

My personal laptop is a Macbook Air. As it also happens, it's the machine on which I happen to be writing this chapter. So for no more reason than the happenstance of my immediate computing environment, I'm going to walk you through installing your XMPP client first on a Mac.

All recent versions of Mac OS X ship with a built-in IM/chat/messaging client named iChat. By a stroke of good fortune, iChat can also function as an XMPP/Jabber client. Configuring it to talk to your new XMPP server is very straightforward.

 At the time I am writing this, Apple is getting ready to release the next version of the Mac OS X operating system: version 10.8, code-named Mountain Lion. Since I'm a member of the Mac OS X developer program, I get to install and play with early releases of new OS updates like Mountain Lion. In fact, as I sit and type these words, I am running Mountain Lion Developer Preview 4.

I tell you all this because in this version of Mac OS, Apple has renamed iChat to Messages. That means that some of my screen shots for this section may look a little different from what you will see when you go to configure iChat on your Mac. None of it should be so different that you have any problems figuring out which fields mean what, but I just thought I'd explain up front why things might not match exactly.

1. Open iChat (or Messages, if you're on Mac OS X 10.8.x).
2. Go into Preferences → Accounts and add a new account.
3. Select Jabber as your account type. This tells the program to use XMPP.
4. For your account name, enter what's known as your Jabber ID (JID). This is *user name@your_XMPP_domain*.

Account Setup

Messages supports AIM, Yahoo!, Google Talk, and Jabber accounts.

Account Type:	Jabber
Account Name:	drensin@exchange.dkrdon
Password:	••••••

▾ Server Options

Server: Auto

Port: Auto   ☑ Use SSL

Use Kerberos v5 for authentication

Cancel   Done

Figure 5-7. Account settings

Remember back in the beginning of this chapter, when I told you that it was absolutely vital to configure your XMPP domain to be the same as the external hostname of your server?

This is why!

Many, though not all, XMPP/Jabber clients derive the server address to which to connect from the information after the @ sign in the JID. In other words, they assume your XMPP domain is the same as the external machine name of the XMPP server. Some, including iChat/Messages, will let you set a specific host separate from your domain, but many will not.

In my case, I configured my XMPP domain to be *exchange.dkrdomain.com*, so that's what comes after the @ sign in my configuration.

5. Enter the Windows Domain password for the user account you're using. (See... I told you integrating the XMPP server with Active Directory would be a good thing!)

6. Lastly, under Server Options, select Use SSL. In the name of good security, you won't allow nonencrypted XMPP traffic in or out of your VPC.

If all goes as it should, you'll hear an audible tone indicating that you've successfully configured your client.

You can skip the next bit about installing on a Windows desktop if you're not using any Windows machines.

Windows

Unlike Mac OS, Windows doesn't come with a default messaging client that understands XMPP/Jabber. There are, however, lots of good third-party clients. One I especially like is Trillian (*http://www.trillian.im*). It's been around a long time, runs on nearly any platform, and has a very nice Web-based client.

I've listed some others for you to consider, too.

Table 5-1. Windows XMPP/Jabber clients

Name	Details
AQQ	aqq.eu (*http://www.aqq.eu/*)
Citron	citron-im.com (*http://www.citron-im.com/*)
Cleartext EIM	cleartext.com (*http://www.cleartext.com/desktop*)
Coccinella	coccinella.im (*http://coccinella.im/*)
Digsby	digsby.com (*http://www.digsby.com/*)
eM Client	emclient.com (*http://www.emclient.com/*)
emesene	emesene.org (*http://blog.emesene.org/*)
Exodus	code.google.com (*http://code.google.com/p/exodus/*)
Gajim	gajim.org (*http://gajim.org/*)
Instantbird	instantbird.com/ (*http://www.instantbird.com/*)
Jabbear	jabbear.com (*http://www.jabbear.com/en/*)
Jabbim	jabbim.com (*http://www.jabbim.com/*)
JAJC	jajc.jrudevels.org (*http://jajc.jrudevels.org/*)
JBuddy Messenger	zionsoftware.com (*http://www.zionsoftware.com/products/messenger/*)
Jeti	jeti-im.org (*http://jeti-im.org/*)
Jitsi (SIP Communicator)	jitsi.org (*http://jitsi.org/*)
Kadu	kadu.net (*http://www.kadu.net/w/English:Main_Page*)
Miranda IM	miranda-im.org (*http://www.miranda-im.org/*)
OneTeam	oneteam.im (*http://oneteam.im/*)
Pandion	pandion.im (*http://pandion.im/*)
Pidgin	pidgin.im (*http://pidgin.im/*)
Psi	psi-im.org (*http://psi-im.org/*)
Psi+	psi-plus.com/ (*http://psi-plus.com/*)
Quiet Internet Pager (QIP)	forum.qip.ru (*http://forum.qip.ru/forumdisplay.php?f=62*)
qutIM	qutim.org (*http://qutim.org/*)
saje	code.google.com (*http://code.google.com/p/saje/*)
SoapBox Communicator	coversant.net (*http://www.coversant.com/products/sbc/*)

Name	Details
Spark	igniterealtime.org (*http://www.igniterealtime.org/projects/spark/*)
Swift	swift.im (*http://swift.im/*)
Tkabber	tkabber.jabber.ru (*http://tkabber.jabber.ru/*)
Tlen	tlen.pl (*http://www.tlen.pl/*)
V&V Messenger	altertech.net (*http://www.altertech.net/products/vv-messenger/*)
Vacuum-IM	vacuum-im.org (*http://www.vacuum-im.org/*)

Configuration varies a bit among these choices, but as long as you remember to enable SSL, you should be OK. (If you have no idea what I'm talking about, then you shouldn't have skipped past the last section on setting up a Mac client. I did warn you!)

Receiving Your First Message

Once you've installed your client of choice, you will want to do a quick check that it's receiving messages correctly.

There are two ways to do this:

- Open a second instance of your client and send yourself a message. This may not be possible with the client you've chosen. It can also get super-confusing fast.
- Use the handy group-send tool built into the Openfire Web administration console.

For my money, the second option wins hands down.

Here's how to do it.

1. Make sure you're logged in to your new XMPP server with your client of choice.
2. Go to the secure Web administrative page on your XMPP server by pointing your browser to `https://your_host:9091`. In my case, that will be *https://exchange.dkrdomain.com:9091*.
3. Log in to the console with the credentials you configured earlier.
4. Click the Sessions tab. You should see your current session listed. If you don't, then make sure your client thinks it's connected to the server.
5. Click the Tools subtab.
6. Enter a test message in the Send Administrative Message text box, and click Send Message.

If everything is working correctly, you should immediately receive your test message on your desktop client.

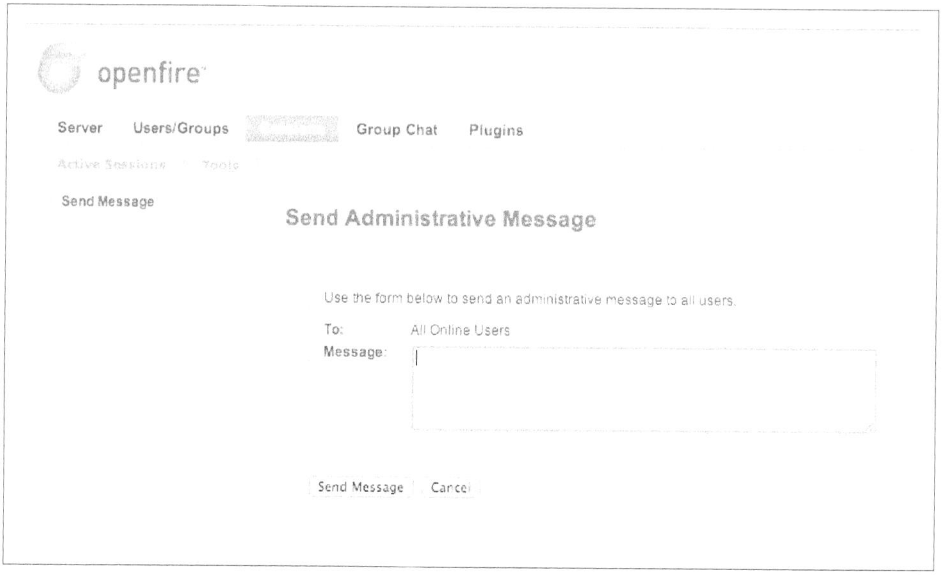

Figure 5-8. Sending your test message

Wrapping Up

Now that you have a working XMPP server, you can do all sorts of really neat things. You have already configured it to get its credentialing information from your Active Directory server, but that's just the beginning.

Hundreds of developers actively contribute to the Openfire project, and they produce some wonderful extensions. For example, in the next chapter, I'm going to help you get your very own voice over IP (VoIP) server set up so you can make phone calls over the Internet. Openfire has an extension that will let your XMPP server talk to your VoIP server, for a truly unified messaging experience.

If you happen to be a software developer—as I am—you now have a wonderful new set of tools to create some really compelling applications. I wrote an XMPP component just a few months ago that lets me control my home thermostat from my IM client. Why? Because I could, and because that's what bored computer geeks like me do.

So, I encourage you to poke, prod, and generally play around with your new XMPP server. Visit the Openfire project page (*http://www.igniterealtime.org/*) and look around a bit at all the neat things you can now do besides basic messaging.

When you're ready, move on to the next chapter, where you'll be taking "messaging" to a whole new level!

## CHAPTER 6

The Voice of a New Generation

Texting, chatting, and email aside, the first killer app of any enterprise is voice.

Traditionally, most or all of the employees of a company sat in the same physical facility and had dedicated desk phones. These phone connected via wires buried in the walls to a central hub called a *Private Branch Exchange* (PBX). The job of the PBX was to route calls between internal phones—i.e., calling someone at their desk using their extension—and shuttling calls to and from the outside world via dedicated phone lines called *trunks*.

Today, most PBXs are digital, and more often than not they are connected via IP to the desktop phone and use the regular office network rather than dedicated wires. You can see how the two approaches differ in the diagram.

The first thing to notice is that a much wider variety of devices are supported by an IP PBX. A traditional system supports only conventional desktop phones, whereas in an IP-based system the phones are really just software clients. That means they can be desktop phones, software clients on PCs, and even clients on mobile devices like smartphones and tablets.

In general, the technologies involved in an IP-based phone system are referred to as Voice Over IP (VoIP). That's the acronym I'll use in this chapter.

Enter SIP

Although several protocols have been proposed over the years for handling phone calls in a VoIP system, the one that dominates the landscape is the Session Initiation Protocol (SIP).

Absolutely every client in a VoIP system—whether a dedicated piece of hardware like a desk phone or a software client on a PC or handheld—understands and uses SIP. You certainly can find other protocols supported by certain software or hardware, but the one thing you can absolutely count on is that whichever device or client you choose, SIP will be one of your options.

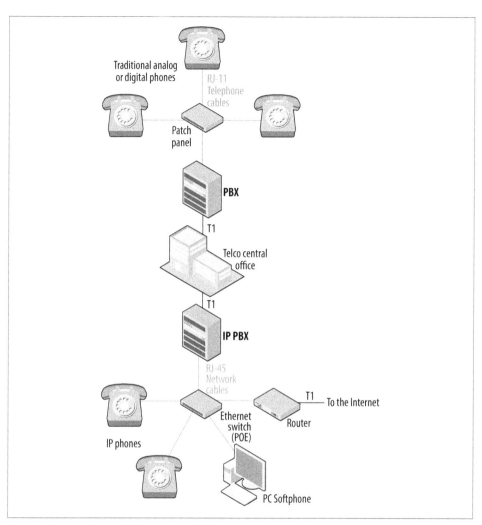

Figure 6-1. A traditional PBX versus an IP-based system

For this reason I'm am going to walk you through installing and configuring your own SIP-based VoIP system.

Among the really great things about a VoIP system is that people don't have to be in the same location in order to talk as if they were. For example, two people could be working at their homes—one with a SIP desk phone and the other with a PC client—and they can dial each other by extension as if they were in the same office. The term "office" is now as much virtual as it is physical.

I'm a good example of this. I keep a very small SIP phone in my bag when I travel. I just plug it into the hotel WiFi network, and when someone dials my extension at work (or calls my direct line), the phone in my hotel room rings. I do the same thing when I'm working from home.

As great as SIP is, it's not without its downsides. The biggest one is that—by default—SIP traffic is not encrypted. That means anyone with a packet sniffer or other network inspection tool who is on the same network as a SIP phone can potentially intercept and listen to calls made to and from that phone.

That's a serious problem!

There are a couple of ways to skin this cat, though. The first is to establish a VPN connection to your infrastructure and run your SIP client/phone over that. If you are using a software phone client (a *softphone*), this should be no problem and all will be right with the world. If, however, you're using a dedicated desk phone, that might not be an option.

The other way to attack the problem is to use an emerging standard called *Secure SIP*. Secure SIP uses most of the same protocols as regular SIP, but adds an encryption layer on top to keep things secure.

Secure SIP is to SIP as HTTPS/SSL is to regular HTTP.

All of this will be covered in great detail when you get to the section on securing your VoIP calls. I just wanted to make sure the issue was in your mind as we proceed.

Picking and Installing a PBX Package

Some software categories have lots of good options from which to choose. Web servers are a good example. You can pick IIS if you prefer a Microsoft platform, use Apache if you prefer a Linux (or other Unix-based) platform, or choose from more than a dozen other potential candidates.

Software PBX, however, is not a category with lots of possible options—especially free ones!

This chapter is going to deviate from the all-Microsoft-all-the-time approach of the previous chapters, because installing a Windows-based PBX is not an option in the Amazon EC2 infrastructure. The Windows Server instances you can set up in EC2 do not have sound drivers installed. You also cannot install a virtual sound driver on these instances. I know this because I spent the better part of two days trying!

Without a sound driver, no PBX is going to work on a Windows instance. That takes Windows—as a server platform for your PBX—off the table for this book and your installation.

If you've never used any operating system other than Windows, you might be inclined to sweat a little bit right now. Don't! I promise you that I've set things up to be as easy as possible for even a complete Linux novice.

The Contenders

Knowing that the PBX is going to run on a Linux instance, you have a few contenders to consider. Although there are more than a few open source projects around that are devoted to creating the perfect PBX on a Linux platform, the overwhelming favorite is a system named Asterisk (*http://www.asterisk.org*).

For all the really wonderful things Asterisk does as a PBX, it needs to be hand-configured using a text editor. It has only a very limited Web GUI.

Not to worry, though. To fill this gap, lots of people have spent incredible amounts of time building easy-to-use front ends for Asterisk. Many of those even come bundled with easy installers. These are known as *distributions*.

Picking an Asterisk Distribution

There is no shortage of products built on top of Asterisk. A *very* partial list of some of the more popular ones includes:

- Asterisk NOW! (*http://www.asterisk.org*)
- FreePBX (*http://www.freepbx.com*)
- Elastix (*http://www.elastix.org*)
- TrixBox (*http://www.trixbox.com*)
- PBX in a Flash (*http://pbxinaflash.net/*)

Each candidate has strengths and weaknesses.

Asterisk Now! is the official distro (that's common shorthand for *distribution*) of the Asterisk project.

FreePBX has the advantage of being largely Asterisk-version neutral, which is to say that it doesn't come bundled with any particular version of Asterisk and is therefore always very quick to work with new versions.

Elastix probably has the most features, including a built-in XMPP server like the one you set up in the last chapter.

TrixBox is very popular because it's easy to install and even easier to maintain.

For complete ease of installation from scratch, however, the hands down winner (in my opinion) is *PBX in a Flash*.

So how do you choose?

If my plan in this chapter was to walk you through installing an Asterisk PBX from scratch, I would strongly recommend PBX in a Flash. Since, however, that is *not* my plan, I'm going to recommend you go in another direction. For the purposes of this chapter I'm assuming:

- You have next to no experience with Linux and aren't necessarily looking for a reason to change that.
- You are interested in the most comprehensive set of features you can get.
- You are looking for something really easy to install, administer, and update.

Given those criteria, I have already prebuilt you a FreePBX EC2 AMI (much like I did for the OpenVPN gateway) that has every bell and whistle I could think of preinstalled for you. It's also running the latest versions (at the time of this writing) of every constituent component.

No, no ... There's no need to name a child after me or throw a parade in my honor. Just recommend this book to everyone you know and we'll call it even!

Installing the PBX

When I created the AMI you are going to use, I did roughly the following:

- Launched a generic Amazon Linux AMI
- Installed a bunch of development-related libraries and software on the instance
- Downloaded, compiled, and installed the necessary sound libraries
- Downloaded, compiled, and installed the most current version of Asterisk
- Downloaded and installed the most current version of FreePBX
- Downloaded, installed, and configured lots of third party add-ons
- Updated all the running components and modules to their most recent stable versions
- Changed the known default passwords and other settings for the Asterisk installation

That might seem like a lot of work—and it was! It took me two straight days to get all of this done and test it for correctness.

Your installation process will, however, look like this:

- Launch a new instance based on an AMI I have already created for you
- Change the passwords I have set up to ones that only you know
- Create and configure a new security group to allow certain traffic

That list should be very manageable for anyone—even if you have zero Linux experience—because all of your administration and configuration will happen through a very friendly Web UI.

All that said, let's dive in.

Finding and launching the instance into the VPC

Go into the EC2 section of the AWS Management Console and launch a new instance. Instead of picking one of the predefined ones from the list, choose the More Amazon Machine Images option.

Figure 6-2. Select a nonstandard image

Be sure to give your instance a meaningful name.

All Linux instances need to be associated with a security key pair. If you don't already have one, just select the Create New option from this screen. If you do opt for a new key pair be *certain* to save it someplace very safe and very memorable on your local machine. You can redownload it if you lose it, but a little caution will save you headaches down the road.

You also have the option of creating your instance with no key pair. That's a terrible idea! The key pair is a much more secure way of connecting to your instance than a regular username/password tuple.

On the next screen, type **DKR** in the search box and select the DKR_PBX image. (This should be familiar to you from earlier in the book.)

Figure 6-3. Choosing the prebuilt PBX image

Like previous instances, you want to be sure to edit the details of this new instance so that they are:

- m1.small
- Launched in your VPC
- In the *default* security group for the VPC

Figure 6-4. Be sure to get the details right!

Next, create a new Elastic IP and assign it to the instance. Finally, create a new VPC security group—I named mine *PBX*—and add a rule to allow TCP port 443 (HTTPS).

Securing the instance

Although I've gone to some trouble to presecure the PBX, there are still a couple of things you *must* immediately do. First, you need to change the default administrator password.

Connect to your new instance via a Web browser using the Elastic IP you just assigned like so:

```
https://your_EIP
```

You will probably get a warning about the security certificate that the Web server is using. It's perfectly fine to keep going. The warning just means that the certificate was self-signed and doesn't come from a trusted CA.

On the screen that follows, click the FreePBX Administration link.

Figure 6-5. *The FreePBX welcome screen*

The next screen is the login screen. The initial credentials are:

- Username: `admin`
- Password: `passw0rd!`

The very first thing you do after logging in with those credentials is *change them*.

In the upper-left corner of the page, select the Admin drop-down and the Administrators option.

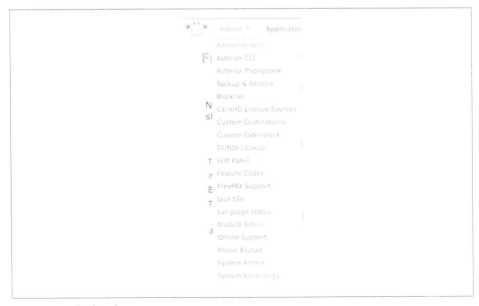

Figure 6-6. *Edit the administrators*

On the screen that follows, select the user named *admin* from the list of users in the upper right of the page.

Figure 6-7. Select the admin user

The left-hand side of the page will show the details for the admin user. Change the entry in the password field to a hard-to-guess password that only *you* know. When you're done, click the Submit Changes button.

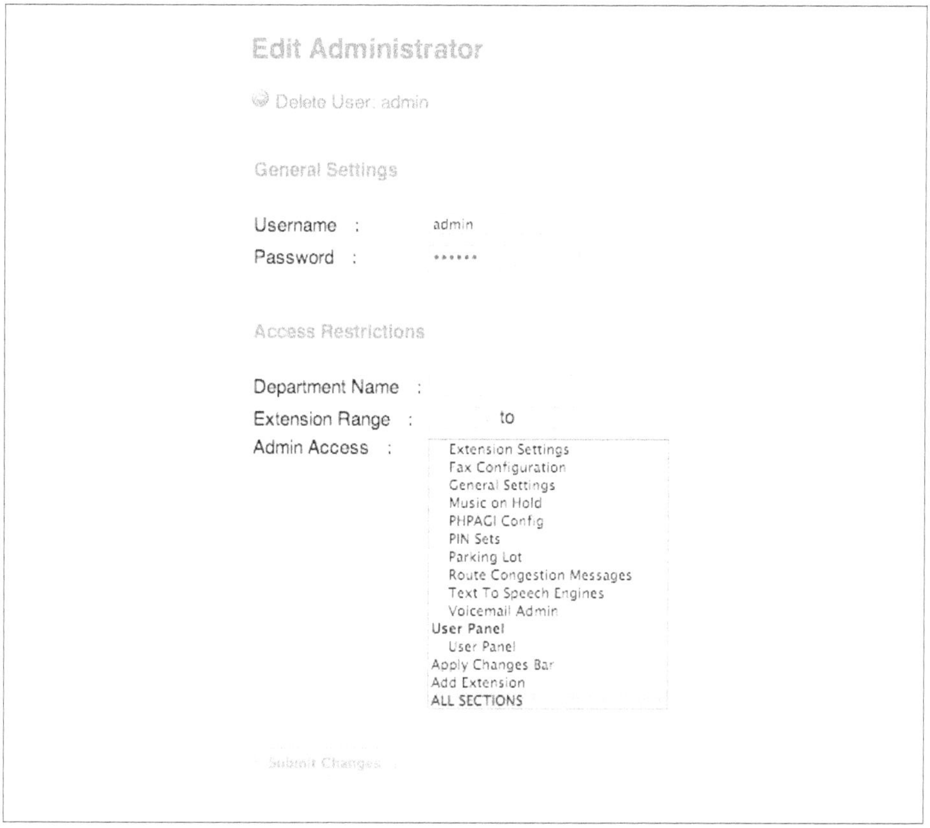

Edit Administrator

⌾ Delete User: admin

General Settings

Username : admin
Password : ······

Access Restrictions

Department Name :
Extension Range : to
Admin Access :

    Extension Settings
    Fax Configuration
    General Settings
    Music on Hold
    PHPAGI Config
    PIN Sets
    Parking Lot
    Route Congestion Messages
    Text To Speech Engines
    Voicemail Admin
    User Panel
    User Panel
    Apply Changes Bar
    Add Extension
    ALL SECTIONS

Submit Changes

Figure 6-8. Change the password and submit changes

Finally, close your browser and log in again with your new credentials.

For the moment, that's all the hardening you need to do. A little later in the chapter I'll cover some other things you need to do to keep your system secure. Before that, however, I need to teach you the basics of your new PBX.

The Basics of Administration and Configuration

Let me start by saying that the Asterisk PBX and the various distros that use it are very deep and rich. Covering even the basics of how a PBX works under the covers, how Asterisk implements those functions, and how to configure a distro like FreePBX to take advantage of those functions could easily occupy another 200+ pages.

My *very* strong recommendation to you is to visit the FreePBX (*http://www.freepbx .com*) site and read the primer articles. They do a good job of explaining the details for which a book like this doesn't have the space.

That said, I can't just throw you to the wolves!

In the pages that follow I will do my best to explain to you the very basics of the system. My goal is that by the end of this chapter you will feel comfortable

- Creating and using new extensions
- Creating and using conference bridges
- Configuring your PBX to handle outbound landline calls
- Using solid encryption to protect the privacy of your calls
- Running the basic administrative tasks necessary to keep your system healthy and safe

Modules

The first concept I'd like to cover is *modules*.

In a nutshell, a module is a piece of software written to hook into the Asterisk system via FreePBX in order to enable a new capability. You can see a list of modules used in your system by clicking the Admin → Module Admin buttons on the main menu bar.

Some of the modules will make immediate sense to you, such as conference bridges, extensions, caller ID, etc. Others won't be so clear. That's not so important right at this moment. The key thing to remember is that nearly everything your system can do is implemented in a module. In fact, the first module I'm going to cover with you is *extensions*.

Extensions

An extension in a software PBX is almost exactly the same thing as an office extension that you should be used to.

As a general rule, computer software tends to expand the limits of the commonplace definitions of things. This is no exception. In truth, lots of things that we wouldn't normally think of in terms of an office extension can—and sometimes are—implemented as "extensions" in Asterisk. For the time being, though, it's perfectly reasonable to think of an Asterisk extension in the same way you would think of a phone extension in your office.

The way you administer extensions in FreePBX is to click the Applications → Extensions menu buttons from the main menu bar.

If you look in the upper-right corner of the page that opens, you will see that I have already created a sample user for you named *John Doe* at extension 001. Go ahead and click on his name to see his details.

There's a lot of information on this page, but I want to highlight just three sections. The first is the general-information section at the top of the page.

Figure 6-9. General information for the extension

The only important part of this section for the moment is the Display Name. You should fill out that field with the name of the person using the extension.

Every extension in your PBX has a specially formatted address that phones and software clients will use to connect directly to it. That format is *extension@address*, where the address can be either the IP address or the DNS hostname of your Asterisk host. In my case, the sample user John Doe can be found at the SIP address *001@pbx.dkrdomain.com*.

It is possible to give your extensions an alias so that they look more like email addresses. For example, I could configure this extension so that people could use *john.doe@pbx.dkrdomain.com* to call John.

The next important section of the extension page is Device Options, which can be found roughly one-third of the way down the page. In particular, you need to pay close attention to the "secret" field. This is the password for the extension.

This device uses sip technology.

secret	abcd1234
dtmfmode	RFC 2833
canreinvite	No
host	dynamic
trustrpid	Yes
sendrpid	No
type	friend
nat	No - RFC3581
port	5060
qualify	yes
qualifyfreq	60
transport	All - TCP Primary
encryption	No
callgroup	
pickupgroup	
disallow	
allow	
dial	SIP/001
accountcode	
mailbox	001@default
vmexten	
deny	0.0.0.0/0.0.0.0
permit	0.0.0.0/0.0.0.0
Custom Context	ALLOW ALL (Default)

Figure 6-10. Make sure to have a strong secret

There are two vital things I cannot stress enough.

- Never, *ever* leave the secret field blank! Under no circumstances is this a reasonable thing to do. All you are doing is inviting people to hack your system.
- *Always* use strong secrets. The example secret I used of `abcd1234` is *not* strong enough. A good password is a mix of upper and lower-case letters, numbers, and at least one punctuation character. For example, `Am3zyQ4@!#P` is a good password to have.

When you are creating your own extensions you should (for the time being) leave everything else in this section alone except the secret.

The next section of this page I would like to focus on is near the bottom and has to do with voice mail.

Voicemail	
Status	Enabled ＊
Voicemail Password	12345
Email Address	john.doe@yourcompany.com
Pager Email Address	
Email Attachment	yes
Play CID	yes
Play Envelope	yes
Delete Voicemail	yes
VM Options	
VM Context	default

Figure 6-11. Voice mail configuration

You can enable voice mail for any extension by changing its status from Disabled to Enabled.

You will, of course, want to enter a voice mail password, or everyone with access to the system will be able to listen to—and delete—the voice mail for this extension.

You can also enable one of my favorite features: voice mail as an email attachment. Just enter a valid email address for the extension and set the Email Attachment toggle to Yes. Whenever this extension gets a voice mail, a copy of it will be sent to the specified email address as an attachment. If you travel a lot, this is a really handy feature because you can check your voice mail right from your email client.

The last thing I would like to say about extensions, before moving on, is that although they have to be numbers, they do not have to start at 1 or be sequential. You will almost certainly want to follow a rule of thumb like, "All user extensions are four digits and conference rooms are five digits," so you can keep your user extensions and your conference bridges grouped together. That said, there's no restriction on how you number them.

Speaking of conference bridges ...

Conference bridges

Although practically everyone hates them, conference calls are a basic fact of life in modern business. It only makes sense for your PBX to accommodate them. Using FreePBX, you can administer your conference bridges from the Applications → Conferences menu item.

Once again I've created a sample conference bridge named Test at extension 1000 to get you started.

Conferences have far fewer options than regular user extensions, but some of them are worth a few words.

User PIN/Admin PIN
> If either of these options is set, anyone calling into the conference will be prompted for a PIN. If User PIN is left blank, callers can just push the # key to enter. The Admin PIN is to make sure that the conference is not actually opened until the admin user has arrived. If Music On Hold is enabled, callers will be placed on hold with music until the admin user comes.

Leader Wait
> When there is an Admin PIN set, the conference won't start until the admin user joins. Callers will just be placed on hold.

Quiet Mode
> Usually, a "bing" noise is played when a user enter or leaves the conference, alerting other members to the fact that someone has joined or left. You can disable that by selecting Yes here.

User Count
> If this is enabled, when someone joins, the conference will say "There are *number* people in this conference."

User Join/Leave
> When people connect to the conference, it will ask them to record their names. The conference will then announce when they join and leave, by name.

Music On Hold
> Enables/disables music on hold for the conference.

Allow Menu
> Allows the users or administrator to press the * key in order to access the conference menu.

Record Conference
> Toggles whether or not to record the conference.

Trunks

A trunk carries a call (or any number of calls) to a Voice-Over-IP Service Provider (VSP) or a device that cares about what number you send to it (e.g., another Asterisk/FreePBX Machine). This installation supports the following types of trunks:

SIP Trunk
> This is by far the most important trunk type for you. Your SIP trunk is what will enable you to call the outside world from your PBX.

Zap Trunk
> These consist of physical hardware that uses the Zapata (*http://www.zapatateleph ony.org/project.html*) interface.

IAX2 Trunk
> This is the *Inter-Asterisk eXchange* protocol native to Asterisk PBX and supported by a number of other soft switches and PBXs. It is used for enabling VoIP connections between servers beside client/server communication. IAX2 is the second generation of this protocol.

ENUM Trunk
> ENUM (E.164 Number to URI Mapping) translates telephone numbers into Internet addresses. You can dial a telephone number and reach a SIP (*http://www .voip-info.org/wiki/view/SIP*), H.323 (*http://www.voip-info.org/wiki/view/H.323*), or any other Internet telephone user. This all happens in the background, so you do not need to do anything special when calling someone. Think of this as the bridge between the switched telephony network and the Internet.

Custom Trunk
> This lets you use a nonstandard (i.e., not SIP or IAX2) protocol to dial calls. You either have to write this trunk code yourself or use someone else's custom trunk.

There is no shortage of third-party SIP trunk providers. In this chapter I'm going to focus on setting up two different SIP trunks: one from a company called SIPStation (*http://www.sipstation.com*) and another using a regular Skype (*http://www.skype .com*) business account.

SIPStation. SIPStation? Who's that?

They're one of dozens of inexpensive VSPs out there. The reason I've elected to focus a bit on them is that they are the easiest to set up using FreePBX. The reason is that the good people at SIPStation have written a module for FreePBX that only requires you to enter an activation key. From that point forward, the module configures every last bit of information your PBX will need in order for you to make and receive calls from regular telephone lines.

You'll sometimes hear or read about regular telephone lines as being *POTS*. That's just an acronym for Plain Old Telephone Service.

Setting up your PBX with SIPStation is very straightforward.

1. Go to the SIPStation home page (*http://www.sipstation.com*) and order a SIP trunk. You will need to get one trunk for every simultaneous outbound call you want to make. In my example, I priced five trunks so my little business could make up to five simultaneous outbound calls to landlines.

2. While you're ordering your trunks, you will want to order at least one DID.

 Direct Inward Dialing (DID) is a service of a local phone company (or local exchange carrier (*http://searchnetworking.techtarget.com/ definition/LEC*)) that provides a block of telephone numbers for calling into a company's PBX system. Using DID, a company can offer its customers individual phone numbers for each person or workstation within the company without requiring a physical line into the PBX for each possible connection.

For example, a company might rent 100 phone numbers from the phone company that could be called over eight physical telephone lines (these are called *trunk lines*). This would allow up to eight ongoing calls at a time; additional inbound calls would get a busy signal until one of the calls completed, or inbound callers could leave a voice mail message. The PBX automatically switches a call for a given phone number to the appropriate workstation in the company. A PBX switchboard operator is not involved.

A DID system can be used for fax (*http://searchnetworking.techtar get.com/definition/fax*) and voice mail as well as for live voice connections. Compared to regular PBX service, DID saves the cost of a switchboard operator, lets calls go through faster, and makes callers feel that they are calling a person rather than a company.

Since I want only one number for my fictitious customers to call (it's OK with me if they get an automated attendant), I've selected only one DID.

Figure 6-12. Ordering trunks and DIDs

3. When you're done ordering, you should see the following information:

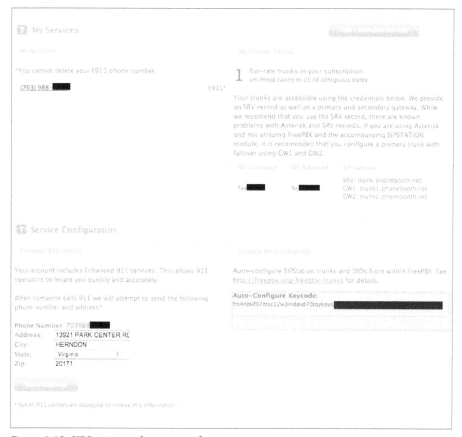

Figure 6-13. SIPStation configuration information

The most important piece of information on this screen is the Auto-Configure Keycode in the bottom right-hand corner. That's the magic code you will use to configure your PBX.

4. Go into your FreePBX administrative page and select Connectivity → SIPSTATION from the menu. On the resulting screen, enter the keycode you just received from SIPStation, click Add Key, and then apply the configuration. In less than 30 seconds your PBX will be completely configured for outbound SIP dialing to any landline via the SIPStation service. Inbound calls will be enabled as well, if you purchased a DID.

Honestly, it can't get any easier than that!

Skype. There are, of course, options other than SIPStation.

Many businesses have corporate Skype accounts for people traveling overseas. What many Skype business account users probably don't know is that Skype also provides VSP services using SIP to its business customers via its Skype Connect (*http://www.skype.com/intl/en-us/business/skype-connect/*) service. This means you can use your existing Skype relationship (though not necessarily exactly your current Skype accounts) to enable your PBX to make outbound calls anywhere in the world.

In this section I'm going to walk you through the process of configuring FreePBX to use Skype as its outbound route to the rest of the world.

First, I'm going to make the assumption that you've already signed up for the Skype Connect service. If you haven't—or don't have ready access—this section is going to be of pretty limited value.

Assuming you're still reading, the very next thing you want to do is add a SIP profile to your Skype Connect account. That's going to mean committing to $6.95/mo for each SIP trunk you want to get from Skype.

For now, just get one.

Once you complete the sign-up, Skype will give you SIP credentials similar to the following:

Figure 6-14. Your Skype SIP profile credentials

Print these or copy them to a handy text file, because you're going to need all of them in this next step. Your Skype SIP Profile credentials are what will enable any VoIP PBX to make calls through the Skype network.

 Don't forget to buy/add credit to your SIP profile. No money means no calls!

Next, open the FreePBX management page and select Connectivity → Trunks → Add a SIP Trunk. Enter the following information:

Trunk Name
    skype-out

Outbound CallerID
    The value from the SIP User field in your Skype SIP Profile

Maximum Channels
    The number of SIP channels you bought

Outgoing Settings

    Trunk Name
        skype-outbound-trunk

    Peer Details

            host=sip.skype.com
            port=5060
            username=*SIP_user*
            secret=*SIP_password*
            canreinvite=no
            type=peer
            nat=yes
            insecure=very

Incoming Settings

    USER Context
        from-trunk

    USER Details

            context=from-trunk
            type=user
            insecure=very
            nat=yes
            canreinvite=no

Register String
    SIP_user:*SIP_password*@sip.skype.com/*SIP_user*

    (for example, 99051000123456:aBcdef3rffasd@sip.skype.com/99051000123456)

Then submit the changes and apply the new configuration.

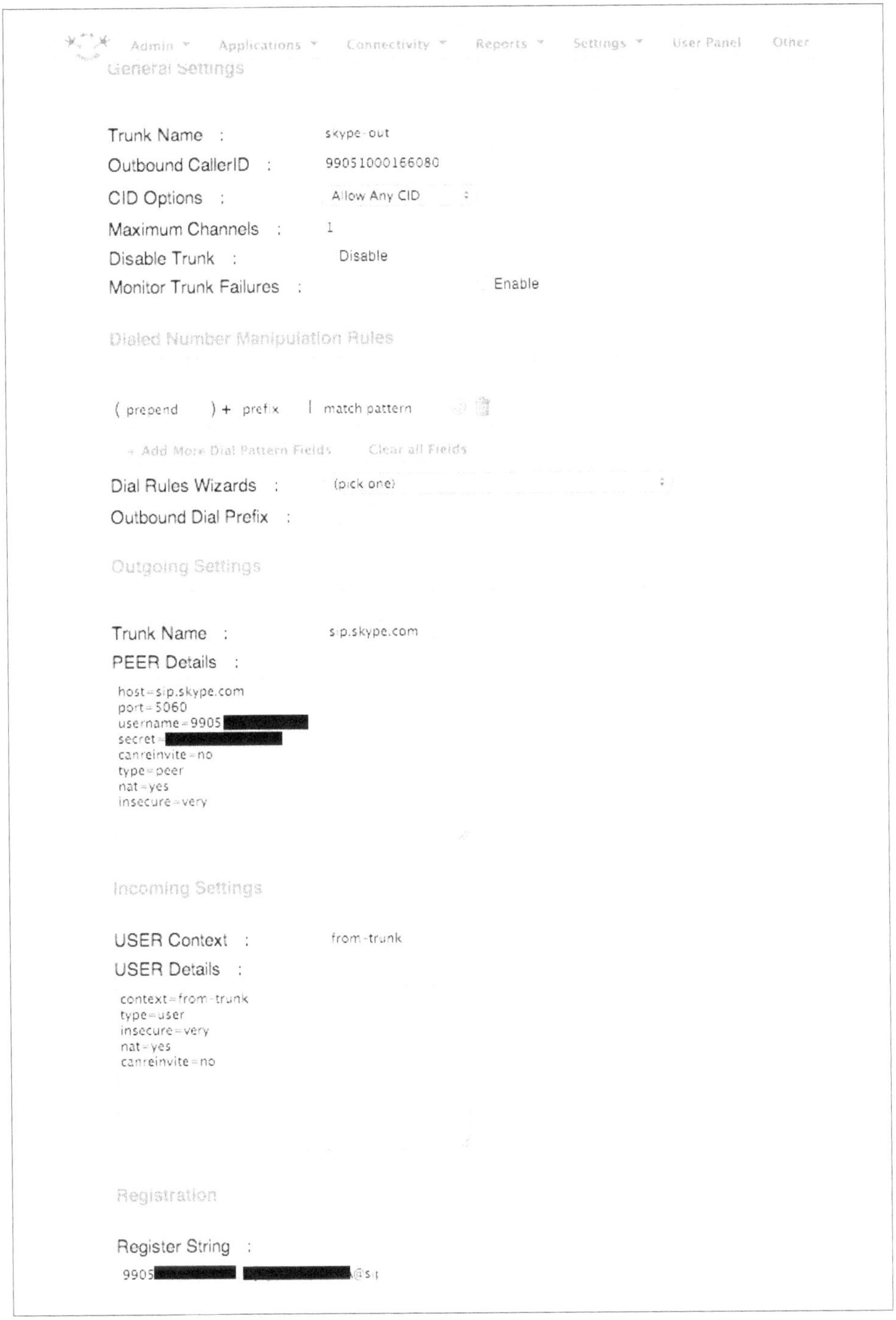

Admin ▾   Applications ▾   Connectivity ▾   Reports ▾   Settings ▾   User Panel   Other

General Settings

Trunk Name :   skype-out
Outbound CallerID :   99051000166080
CID Options :   Allow Any CID ▾
Maximum Channels :   1
Disable Trunk :   Disable
Monitor Trunk Failures :   Enable

Dialed Number Manipulation Rules

(prepend   ) + prefix | match pattern   ⤵ 🗑

+ Add More Dial Pattern Fields   Clear all Fields

Dial Rules Wizards :   (pick one)   ▾
Outbound Dial Prefix :

Outgoing Settings

Trunk Name :   sip.skype.com
PEER Details :

host=sip.skype.com
port=5060
username=9905▓▓▓▓▓▓▓▓▓
secret=▓▓▓▓▓▓▓▓▓▓▓▓
canreinvite=no
type=peer
nat=yes
insecure=very

Incoming Settings

USER Context :   from-trunk
USER Details :

context=from-trunk
type=user
insecure=very
nat=yes
canreinvite=no

Registration

Register String :
9905▓▓▓▓▓▓ ▓▓▓▓▓▓▓▓▓▓@s p

Figure 6-15. Your completed trunk

You're almost done. Now select Connectivity → Outbound Routes from the main menu. You should already see one outbound route in the upper right-hand corner. Select that.

All you have to do on this page is go to the very bottom and make sure that you select your "skype-out" trunk for slot 0 in the outbound trunk sequence section. Then just submit changes and apply!

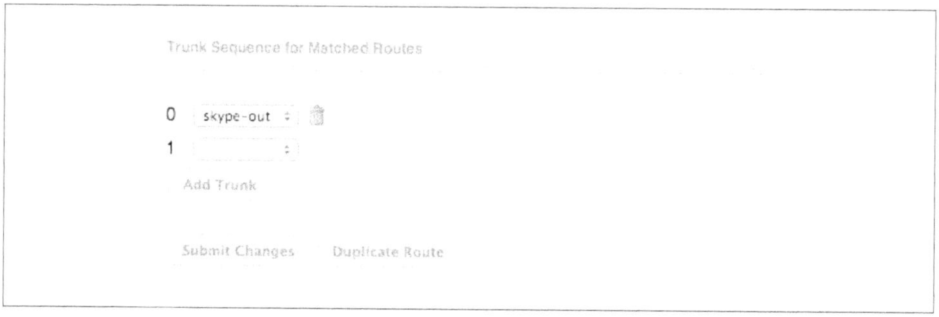

Figure 6-16. The correct trunk sequence

I know that's a lot of steps to follow, so let me take a moment and explain each part.

The meat of what you just did is in the Peer Details section of your new Skype SIP trunk. You entered the following:

```
host=sip.skype.com
port=5060
username=SIP_user
secret=SIP_password
canreinvite=no
type=peer
nat=yes
insecure=very
```

The host, port, username, and secret entries should require no explanation at this point. The other four entries, however, do.

canreinvite=no

When SIP initiates the call, the INVITE message contains the information about where to send the media streams. Asterisk uses itself as the endpoints of media streams when setting up the call. Once the call has been accepted, Asterisk sends another (re)INVITE message to the clients with the information necessary to have the two clients send the media streams directly to each other.

canreinvite=no stops the sending of the (re)INVITEs once the call is established.

Generally, the reason to use this option is that some third-party hardware do not handle (re)INVITEs well and can result in crashes. Since you will never know what hardware Skype is using for its SIP service or when it might change, this option protects you from that prospect.

type=peer

Asterisk requires the relationship type between the two connecting systems to be explicitly defined. Since Asterisk 1.2 the developers have strongly advised that you use peer in this case. The reason is as much historical as anything else, but the point that's most important to you is that you be sure to use this specific value. The basic takeaway is that Asterisk initiates a call to a SIP *peer* but accepts a call from a SIP *user*.

nat=yes

Configured as a peer, this setting causes Asterisk to ignore the address information in the SIP and Session Description Protocol (SDP) headers from this peer, and reply to the sender's IP address and port. nat=yes enables a form of Symmetric RTP (*http://www.voip-info.org/wiki/view/RTP+Symmetric*) and SIP Comedia mode (*http://www.cisco.com/en/US/docs/ios/voice/sip/configuration/guide/sip_cg-com _fork_mlpp.html*) in Asterisk.

Comedia mode means that Asterisk will ignore the IP and port in the received SDP from the peer and will wait for an incoming Real-time Transport Protocol (RTP) packet. This RTP should arrive to the port that Asterisk replied in the "200 OK" SDP. After that, Asterisk already knows where to send its RTP.

The important thing to remember is that this option causes the PBX to ignore any redirect attempts from the peer. This is desirable for two reasons:

- It's preferable from a security standpoint.
- It forces you to be explicit about the peering information, which is just good practice.

insecure=very

In light of the previous passage, this line might seem just a bit contradictory! Allow me to explain.

This option just says that Skype won't have to reauthenticate to your PBX as a registered user in order to transfer in-bound calls. The only reason I even included it in the configuration at all is because there have been reports on various Internet sites and forums that without it, users have experienced intermittent dropped calls.

In the user details section I had you enter:

```
context=from-trunk
type=user
insecure=very
nat=yes
canreinvite=no
```

The last three entries you already know. The first two, however, need a little color.

context=from-trunk

Unknown SIP callers (which is what Skype callers will be) need to go to the from-trunk context instead of the normal from-sip-external context. This line is essentially acknowledging that the inbound call will be unauthenticated and making sure to route it internally in Asterisk via a path that won't cause it to be rejected.

type=user

A SIP *user* is a construct from which the PBX *accepts* a call. A *peer* is something to which the PBX *places* a call. Incoming calls, by definition, are users and not peers.

Configuring Secure SIP with TLS and SRTP

One of the big knocks against VoIP in general and the SIP protocol specifically is that calls are unencrypted. This means someone sitting between your client and your PBX could potentially eavesdrop on your conversations. That's clearly no good!

The response to these concerns is to use an existing encryption protocol (Transport Layer Security, or TLS), create a new encrypted media protocol (Secure Real-time Transport Protocol, or SRTP), and use them together to secure VoIP calls. A secure call happens as follows:

1. The VoIP client software/hardware attempts to establish an encrypted network session to the PBX—usually on port 5061—using the TLS protocol.

2. If the connection is successful, the encrypted channel is used to send the SIP registration/authorization credentials to the PBX so that the client can be validated as a trusted user.

3. The PBX and the client then negotiate which UDP ports they're going to use for the actual audio channels. Your PBX is set up to negotiate for ports in the range of 10000–20000.

4. The audio packets for the session are encrypted via the SRTP protocol and the conversation continues until somebody hangs up.

As a good rule of thumb, you want to allow only software and hardware that support TLS/SRTP to connect to your PBX. Allowing unencrypted traffic is asking to be hacked.

Setting up FreePBX/Asterisk to support encrypted calls isn't very hard if you know the magic words. If you don't (as I didn't when I started writing this chapter), it can be a royal pain!

Your PBX is already set up to handle secure calls. You only have to remember to set up your extensions to use encryption. Otherwise they won't be able to register with the system.

To set up encryption, open the page for the example extension 001. In the Device Options section, change the values `transport` to **TLS Only** and encryption to **Yes (SRTP only)**.

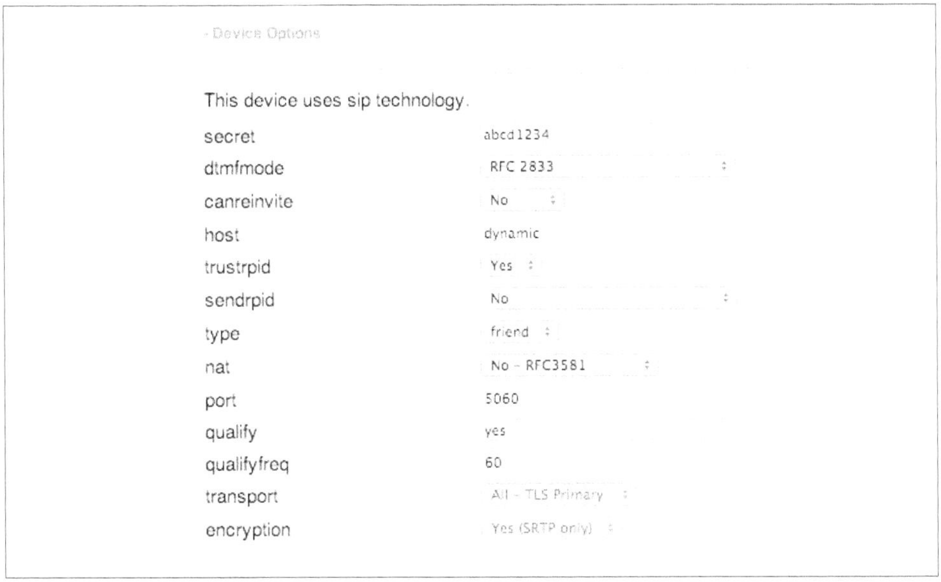

Figure 6-17. Extension encryption settings

What you've just done is told the PBX that anyone trying to authenticate using extension 001 *must* do so via TLS encryption and can conduct audio sessions only via encrypted SRTP.

As long as you remember to set those fields as you are creating or changing your extensions, you should have no problems.

Detecting and dealing with hacking attempts

VoIP, like most applications, likes to use a set of standard ports. In this case, a standard unencrypted SIP session starts on UDP port 5060. Because this is a well-known port, attackers will try to gain entry into your system through it. You have three choices in preventing attacks:

1. Make sure all your extensions use very strong passwords and don't worry about it.
2. Change your default SIP port.
3. Don't allow *any* unencrypted data into your PBX.

Lest there be any confusion, I'm going to strongly recommend option 3!

Even if you don't let unencrypted SIP into your PBX, attackers will still try to break in. As an extra measure of protection, it's a good idea to use some sort of intrusion-detection software. The application most commonly used in the Asterisk community to detect and punish people trying to hack into your system is a module named *fail2ban*.

In a nutshell, fail2ban keeps track of IP addresses that fail to successfully register with the PBX, and after a certain number of failures, bans them for a specified amount of time.

fail2ban is already installed and running on your PBX. Tweak its settings by choosing Admin → System Admin → Intrusion Detection.

Status: running

Intrusion Detection   Stop   Restart

Ban Time: 1800

Max Retry: 8

Find Time: 600

E-mail:

                127.0.0.1

Whitelist

Banned IP's

Submit

Figure 6-18. fail2ban settings

 Be sure to enter your email address on the Intrusion Detection page so that you get email messages when fail2ban detects people trying to break into your system.

Configuring the Network for VoIP

The last thing you need to do before you can start using your PBX to make calls is to configure your network settings.

1. Choose Settings → Asterisk SIP Settings. At the top of the page, click the button marked Auto Configure. This ensures that your PBX knows what its external IP address is: the one you got when you allocated the Elastic IP earlier. This is vital for the audio packets to actually flow correctly in and out of the PBX.

2. Earlier you created a security group named *PBX* that had one rule in it, to allow HTTPS traffic so you could use the Web administrative interface. Now you need to add two more rules:

   a. Allow inbound TCP on port 5061. This is the port for the TLS negotiation.

b. Allow inbound UDP on ports 10000–20000. These will be used for the SRTP media.

That's it! You are now ready to start making test calls,

Making VoIP Calls

It goes without saying that in order to make VoIP calls, you first need to install some VoIP software. In this section I'll walk you through a couple of my favorites.

Blink (PC/Mac)

There are tons of VoIP clients for the PC and Mac. My personal favorite is one called Blink. You can download it for free from the Blink download page (*http://icanblink.com/download.phtml*). Go ahead and install the client.

In the Preferences section, add an account. Remember that your SIP address is *001@external_IP_address_of_your_PBX*. Mine is *001@pbx.dkrdomain.com*.

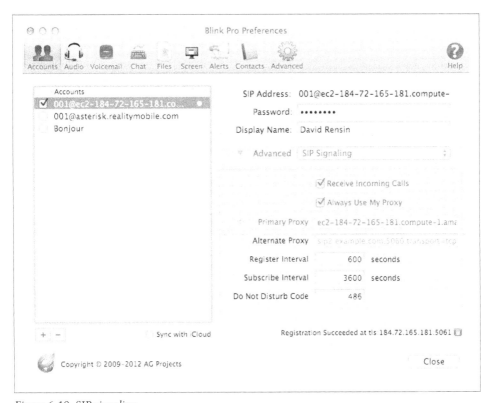

Figure 6-19. SIP signaling

After you've entered your SIP name and password, you will need to change a few of the default settings in order to make encrypted calls.

In the SIP Signaling section you need to set your Primary Proxy to *your_exter nal_PBX_IP_address:5061;transport=tls*. Note the use of the colon and semicolon. This string tells Blink that it shouldn't try to guess your PBX from your SIP address, but instead should always connect to your account at your Elastic IP address using TLS on port 5061.

In the RTP Media section of your configuration, set SRTP Encryption to "mandatory."

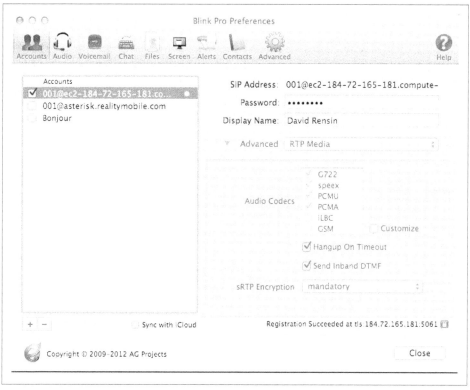

Figure 6-20. SRTP Encryption

Now you should be ready to go. Click Close, and the main Blink window should show you as being securely registered to the PBX.

Time to make your first test call!

The sequence ***65** will tell you what your current extension is, so go ahead and dial that. If things are configured correctly, you should hear a voice prompt say:

"Your extension is 0-0-1."

Take special care to note the encryption indicators in the call user interface.

Figure 6-21. Your first encrypted call

The blue lock icon means you're using TLS for registration and authentication. The orange icon means you're using SRTP for the voice data.

Bria (iPhone/iPad/Android)

CounterPath (*http://www.counterpath.com/products.html*) makes a very nice client for iOS and Android devices named Bria. It's not free, but it is pretty cheap and works really well. The Android version cost me $8.95.

The only two things to watch out for with Bria are:

1. Make sure you enable calling via mobile data in the main Bria preferences.
2. Be sure to select TLS and SRTP mandatory encryption from the advanced section of your account preferences.

Other than that, it couldn't be any easier!

Wrapping Up

It ain't what you don't know that gets you into trouble.
It's what you know for sure that just ain't so.

—Mark Twain

I'll let you in on a little secret.

When I started this chapter I thought I knew a lot about configuring the Asterisk PBX and FreePBX interfaces. Boy, was I wrong!

I've done my level best to make installing and running your PBX as simple as possible, so you won't have to face the same hurdles I did. That said, I should caution you in the strongest terms that this new PBX of yours is one very powerful beast. There are literally thousands of pages of documentation (and probably tens of thousands of pages of unofficial documentation) on how to compile, configure, maintain, and otherwise pimp out an Asterisk system.

The information in this chapter should be just the beginning of your learning about this system. I *strongly* encourage you to go through the various getting-started guides found on the main FreePBX and Asterisk sites. They are invaluable resources and will fill in a lot of gaps for you.

This chapter also represents the most complicated thing you've done (or will do) in this book. The remaining chapters are pretty tame in comparison to this.

So take a deep breath, limber up a little, and let's head into the home stretch ...

## CHAPTER 7

Keeping Your Network Fit, Trim, and Healthy

Setting up your network to work exactly the way you want it to is one thing. Keeping it running smoothly is something different altogether.

In this chapter I'll walk you through some of the basics of keeping your network running smoothly, and making sure that if a catastrophe hits you'll still be up and running. All of these topics are important no matter what infrastructure you're using, though some of the details are specific to the Amazon Web Services cloud.

All of these topics are also highly automatable, so you don't have to spend valuable time performing them manually.

Regular Backups

If the first rule of real estate is *location, location, location*, the first rule of IT should be *backup, backup, backup*.

The good news is that creating backups in the AWS cloud is about as simple as humanly possible. All you have to do is choose an instance and create a *snapshot*—which is exactly what it sounds like—a perfect copy of your instance at a specific moment in time.

Then you can go in periodically and clean out snapshots you don't need.

It couldn't get any easier, right?

Well, actually ... it kind of *could*.

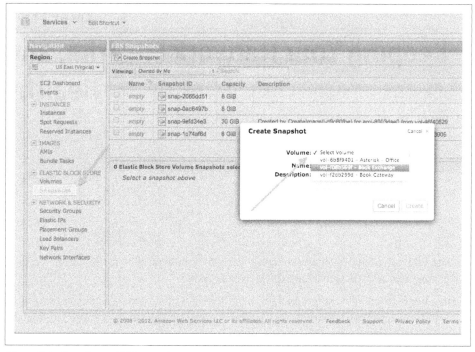

Figure 7-1. Creating an EC2 snapshot

Automated EC2 Backups

"Introducing the EC2 API Command Line Tools" on page 73 introduced some of the really cool command-line tools Amazon provides. One of the things I didn't tell you was that if you create a server based on one of the AWS stock instance types, the tools are automatically installed for you on the instance. Up until now that hasn't been particularly useful to know.

Of course, if you happen to be using an image that doesn't have the tools installed, you can always refer back to Chapter 4 to learn how to install them.

One of the command-line tools that I didn't cover earlier is `ec2-create-snapshot`. This lets you create your own scripts to run periodically to take snapshots of your production instances.

The syntax of `ec2-create-snapshot` is:

```
ec2-create-snapshot volume_id [-d description]
```

The options in this string are:

volume_id
> The ID of the Amazon EBS volume to take a snapshot of, such as `vol-4d826724`.

description

A description you want to give the snapshot, maybe something like `daily backup`.

As with the other EC2 API command-line tools, you will need your private key and certificate file that you downloaded and saved in a safe place from Chapter 4. The other important options for this command are shown in Table 7-1.

Table 7-1. ec2-create-snapshot options

Option	Description
`--region` *region*	Overrides the region specified in the EC2_URL environment variable and the URL specified by the -U option. Default: The value of the EC2_URL environment variable, or `us-east-1` if EC2_URL isn't set.
	Example: `--region eu-west-1`
`-U, --url` *url*	The uniform resource locator (URL) of the Amazon EC2 web service entry point.
	Default: The value of the EC2_URL environment variable, or *https://ec2.amazonaws.com* if EC2_URL isn't set.
	Example: `-U https://ec2.amazonaws.com`
`-K, --private-key` *ec2-private-key*	The private key that identifies you to Amazon EC2. For more information, see Tell the Tools Who You Are (*http://docs.amazonwebservices.com/AWSEC2/latest/UserGuide/setting-up-your-tools.html#set-aws-credentials*).
	Default: The value of the EC2_PRIVATE_KEY environment variable. If EC2_PRIVATE_KEY isn't set, you must specify this option.
	Example: `-K pk-HKZYKTAIG2ECMXYIBH3HXV4ZBEXAMPLE.pem`
`-C, --cert` *ec2-cert*	The X.509 certificate that identifies you to Amazon EC2.
	Default: The value of the EC2_CERT environment variable. If EC2_CERT isn't set, you must specify this option.
	Example: `-C cert-HKZYKTAIG2ECMXYIBH3HXV4ZBEXAMPLE.pem`

The following three-line batch file is an example that you can run in Windows as a scheduled job to back up three production instances.

```
ec2-create-snapshot vol-f2db299d -d "%DATE% - Gateway Backup" -K pk-
HKZYKTAIG2ECMXYIBH3HXV4ZBEXAMPLE.pem -C cert-HKZYKTAIG2ECMXYIBH3HXV4ZBEXAMPLE.pem
ec2-create-snapshot vol-f08b569f -d "%DATE% - Exchange Backup" -K pk-
HKZYKTAIG2ECMXYIBH3HXV4ZBEXAMPLE.pem -C cert-HKZYKTAIG2ECMXYIBH3HXV4ZBEXAMPLE.pem
ec2-create-snapshot vol-6h8f9401 -d "%DATE% - PBX Backup" -K pk-
HKZYKTAIG2ECMXYIBH3HXV4ZBEXAMPLE.pem -C cert-HKZYKTAIG2ECMXYIBH3HXV4ZBEXAMPLE.pem
```

Now backing up is as easy as humanly possible! Right?

Almost!

One of the great programmers of Unix lore (and the inventor of the popular Perl language), Larry Wall (*http://en.wikipedia.org/wiki/Larry_Wall*), is famous for having observed that a good programmer possesses three vital attributes: *laziness*, *impatience*, and *hubris*.

As it happens, I'm a programmer by trade, not a regular IT person. That means I'm always looking for easier ways to do things. Sure, I could leave this section as is and let you fend for yourself, but there's an even *easier* way to handle your backups.

From the moment Amazon announced its AWS services, several companies sprang up, aiming to help you manage your cloud assets. One of the biggest is RightScale (*http://www.rightscale.com*). Its service lets you do all kinds of wonderfully useful things around your cloud assets. RightScale isn't restricted to AWS, either. It can handle pretty much every major cloud provider.

RightScale isn't alone, either. Dozens of vendors do similar things. Most, however, suffer from two problems,

- They can get pretty expensive, scaring you off if you're a tightwad like me.
- They do a lot of stuff. In fact, for this particular network and this particular book, they do a little *too* much. If you're just starting out, a service like that is a bit of a Swiss army chainsaw.

All you really need for the infrastructure you've constructed so far is a simple service to automate the creation and pruning of snapshots. The cheaper, the better.

Enter my new favorite cloud-related service: AutoSnappy (*http://www.autosnappy .com*). For $3 per month it will run, monitor, and prune as many snapshots as you like.

All you need to do is register an account, provide the information requested, agree to the monthly billing, and set up your automated jobs. The only tricky bit about it—and it's not *that* tricky—is that when you create a new job you have to specify it in `cron` format. `cron` is a tool found on Unix-style systems like Linux, FreeBSD, and others. It lets you set up tasks to run at specific times, or intervals. The AutoSnappy service uses a pretty simple `cron` format. The format consists of five fields, each delimited by a space.

Both numbers and ranges of numbers are allowed. Ranges are two numbers separated with a hyphen. The specified range is inclusive. For example, `8-11` for an `hours` entry specifies execution at hours 8, 9, 10 and 11.

Any field may be an asterisk (*), which always stands for "first to last" or "run every time." Thus, an asterisk in the fourth field causes the script to run once per hour.

The cron File Format

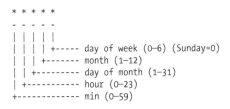

```
* * * * *
- - - - -
| | | | |
| | | | +----- day of week (0-6) (Sunday=0)
| | | +------- month (1-12)
| | +--------- day of month (1-31)
| +----------- hour (0-23)
+------------- min (0-59)
```

Lists are allowed. A list is a set of numbers separated by commas. Examples: 1,2,5,9 and 0,3,4.

Example:

```
20,40 5-8 20-30 * *
```

This means:

20,40
    Run when the minute is 20 or 40

5-8
    of 5 through 8 a.m.

20-30
    during the 20th through 30th day

*
    of each month

*
    no matter what day of the week it is

This implementation allows only day-of-week or day-of-month to be specified. One or the other (or both) must be *.

Using AutoSnappy, I set up a job in less than 5 minutes that:

- Creates new snapshots at 3 a.m. every day
- Deletes old snapshots at 4 a.m. every day
- Checks that I have at least one snapshot, but not more than 10, every day at 5 a.m. and alerts me if there's a problem.

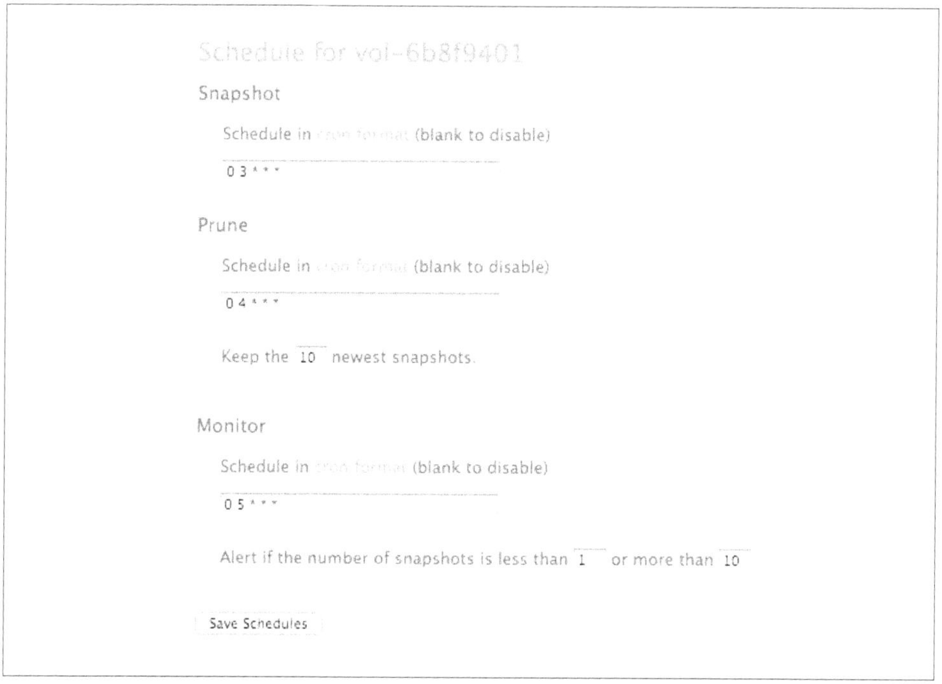

Figure 7-2. The snapshot schedule for one of my volumes

Now it's as simple as possible!

Monitoring

Restoring from a backup in the event of a disaster is all well and good, but a well-built IT infrastructure is monitored continuously to try and spot problems *before* they become disasters.

For the purpose of monitoring your AWS-based infrastructure, Amazon introduced a service called *CloudWatch (https://console.aws.amazon.com/cloudwatch/)*. As of this writing there are nearly 500 metrics you can watch using the CloudWatch dashboard. You can set alerts on these metrics, as well. They include everything you might expect —such as CPU utilization and disk I/O—and some metrics you may not expect, like billing and usage alerts.

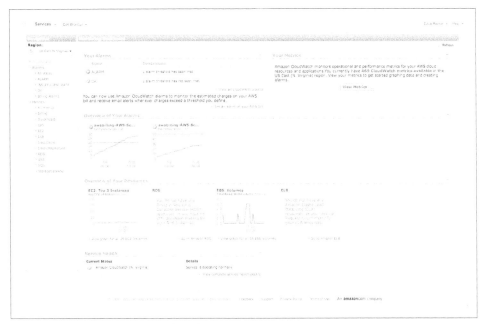

Figure 7-3. The CloudWatch dashboard

To get started, you should enable detailed monitoring on all your instances. This was an option when you launched them, but I asked you to ignore it. Now it's time to use it.

To enable detailed monitoring for a specific instance, simply right-click it in the EC2 management page, and select Enable Detailed Monitoring. Now, when you look at the *Monitor* tab of the details pane for an instance, you will see several stock graphs. If you click one, you will see a more detailed view. The place to go for metrics is the Cloud-Watch (*https://console.aws.amazon.com/cloudwatch/*) dashboard page. From there you can select all sorts of interesting metrics and create alerts on them.

For example, from that page I created email alerts when my monthly estimated bill exceeded $20, $50, and $100.

In any case, the interface is very intuitive, and you should have no problem setting up your own metrics and alerts.

It's easy to blow off the monitoring aspect of running a network, but resist the urge. At a minimum, set alerts for all your instances for when CPU utilization exceeds 90 percent and network bandwidth exceeds 50 percent. Those two simple things will let you get to an instance before it falls over from load.

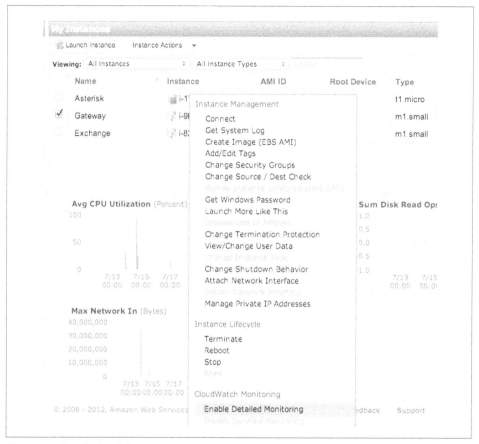

Figure 7-4. Enable detailed monitoring

System Updates

To keep your machine instances running smoothly, you need to automatically update the software running on them. For your Windows instances, this is easy. Just RDP to each instance and enable Windows Update to automatically run and install updates at a convenient time—like 3 a.m. every day.

Your PBX instance is a tiny bit more difficult.

SSH: Your New Best Friend

The Linux-based instances in your infrastructure have no installed GUI; all the administrative functions need to be performed from the command line. If you're not an experienced Linux user you probably don't know how to do this.

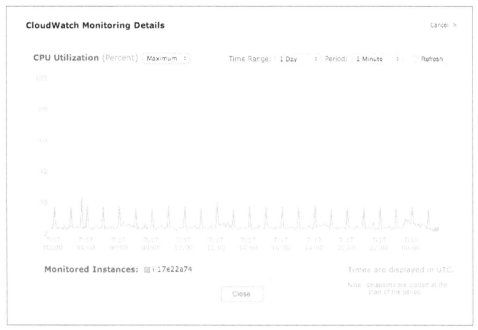

Figure 7-5. CPU utilization for the PBX

The first thing to do is to establish a secure link to the instance and get a command prompt so you can perform your administration. This is done via a protocol called *Secure Shell* or *SSH*.

If you're on a Mac—as I am—you already have an SSH client built into your operating system. If you're on a Windows machine, you will need to download a third-party SSH client. The one nearly everybody on the planet seems to use is *PuTTY*. You can download it directly from the developer (*http://the.earth.li/~sgtatham/putty/latest/x86/putty -0.62-installer.exe*).

SSH connections are secured in one of two ways: with a client security certificate or with a username and password. *All* EC2 Linux instances are secured via a special certificate that is unique to your account. You may recall that when you first launched your Asterisk instance in the previous chapter, you were prompted for a security key pair. You may also recall that I asked you to use the value already provided to you and to *never* launch a new Linux-based instance without a key pair.

Here's where that pays off.

If you didn't heed my advice and save your key pair at the time you created your instance, you're in for a bumpy ride. There's no way to recover a missing key pair after you launch your instance. This is why I was so adamant about you storing this file in a place you could return to easily.

If you *do* find yourself in this unfortunate position, the easiest thing to do is:

1. Create an AMI from your instance.
2. Terminate your instance.
3. Launch a new instance based on your newly created AMI and tell Amazon you want a new key pair file.
4. Be sure to launch it into your VPC!
5. Save the key pair someplace safe!!!

Assuming you have your key pair handy, here's how to attach to your PBX command line.

From a Mac or Linux Machine

From a terminal window, type the following command:

```
ssh -i path_to_your_keypair_file ec2-user@elastic_ip_address_or_hostname_of_your_pbx
```

For me that looks like:

```
ssh -i dkr-ec2.pem ec2-user@pbx.dkrdomain.com
```

 The more experienced among you might be wondering why we're connecting as the user ec2-user and not as root. All Amazon stock Linux AMIs want you to use the default—nonprivileged—user ec2-user and then use sudo for any privileged commands you may need to execute.

If all goes well, you should be at a command prompt similar to this:

```
Last login: Tue Jul 17 00:45:30 2012 from c-68-57-108-122.hsd1.va.comcast.net

       _|  _|_  )
       _|  (     /   Amazon Linux AMI
       ___|\___|___|

See /usr/share/doc/system-release/ for latest release notes.
There are 41 security update(s) out of 230 total update(s) available
Amazon Linux version 2012.03 is available.
[ec2-user@domU-12-31-39-14-14-AA ~]$
```

From Windows

Download and install PuTTY (*http://the.earth.li/~sgtatham/putty/latest/x86/putty-0.62-installer.exe*).

The first thing you have to do is to convert the *.pem* key pair that you saved from Amazon into a PuTTY-specific format known as a *.ppk*. To do this:

1. Open PutTTYgen from your Start menu.
2. Click File → Load Private Key and select the *.pem* file you downloaded. (Be sure to change the filename filter from ***.ppk** to ***.*** in order to find your file.)
3. Click the Save Private Key button and save your new *.ppk* file someplace you will remember.
4. Close PuTTYgen.

Now that you have your key pair in a format that PuTTY can understand, you can configure and connect to your PBX machine.

1. Open PuTTY from the Start Menu.
2. In the Host Name field, put the Elastic IP address of your server.
3. Under Connection → SSH → Auth, browse for your new *.ppk* file.
4. Back in the Session tree item, enter a name for your configuration in the Saved Sessions text box and click Save.
5. Click Open to connect to your PBX.
6. When the terminal window opens, you will be prompted with `login as`. Enter the user **ec2-user**.

You should see the following output in your terminal window:

```
login as: ec2-user
Authenticating with public key "imported-openssh-key"
Last login: Wed Jul 18 18:11:27 2012 from wsip-98-173-183-2.dc.dc.cox.net
```

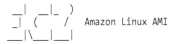

```
       __|  __|_  )
       _|  (     /   Amazon Linux AMI
      ___|\___|___|
```

```
https://aws.amazon.com/amazon-linux-ami/2012.03-release-notes/
[ec2-user@ip-10-0-0-173 ~]$
```

When you're done with your session just type **exit** at the prompt and the window will close. From now on, when you want to connect via SSH to your PBX, just run PuTTY and load the session you just saved.

Setting Up Daily Updates

Now that you're connected to your instance via SSH, here's how to set up system updates to run every day.

1. Execute `sudo -i` to get to a root prompt.

 If you're not familiar with Unix-style systems, the user root is the same as Administrator on a Windows machine. That account has access to absolutely every aspect of the machine.

2. Enter the following command:

   ```
   cd /etc/cron.daily
   ```

   This puts you in the *cron.daily* directory, which contains scripts to run daily on the instance.

3. Enter the following command:

   ```
   echo "#! /bin/sh" >> upgrade.sh; echo "yum -y update" >>
                            upgrade.sh; chmod +x upgrade.sh
   ```

   This long command is actually three commands bundled together. The first two (which start with `echo`) create a new text file called *upgrade.sh* that contains the following two lines:

   ```
   #! /bin/sh
   yum -y update
   ```

   This script uses the built-in system software installer—yum—to apply all the available system and software updates without prompting the user for permission.

   The last of the three commands—`chmod +x upgrade.sh`—makes the text file an executable script file.

4. Run `./upgrade.sh` to test your upgrade script and make sure it really updates the system. If it works, you'll see a listing similar to this:

   ```
   Loaded plugins: fastestmirror, priorities, security, update-motd
   Loading mirror speeds from cached hostfile
    * amzn-main: packages.us-east-1.amazonaws.com
    * amzn-updates: packages.us-east-1.amazonaws.com
   amzn-main                                          | 2.1 kB     00:00
   amzn-updates                                       | 2.3 kB     00:00
   Setting up Update Process
   Resolving Dependencies
   --> Running transaction check
   ---> Package acl.x86_64 0:2.2.49-4.8.amzn1 will be updated
   ---> Package acl.x86_64 0:2.2.49-6.9.amzn1 will be an update
   ---> Package alsa-lib.x86_64 0:1.0.21-3.8.amzn1 will be updated

   ...

   ---> Package kernel.x86_64 0:2.6.35.14-97.44.amzn1 will be erased
   ```

```
---> Package kernel-devel.x86_64 0:2.6.35.14-97.44.amzn1 will be erased
--> Finished Dependency Resolution

Dependencies Resolved

================================================================================
 Package                  Arch    Version                      Repository    Size
================================================================================
Installing:
 generic-logos            noarch  16.0.0-1.4.amzn1             amzn-updates  588 k
     replacing  system-logos.noarch 4.9.99-11.13.amzn1
 jpackage-utils           x86_64  1.7.5-15.16.amzn1            amzn-main      77 k
     replacing  jpackage-utils.noarch 1.7.5-3.12.13.amzn1
 kernel                   x86_64  3.2.22-35.60.amzn1           amzn-updates  8.6 M
 kernel-devel             x86_64  3.2.22-35.60.amzn1           amzn-updates  7.3 M
 mysql51                  x86_64  5.1.61-4.54.amzn1            amzn-updates  1.1 M
     replacing  mysql.x86_64 5.1.61-1.27.amzn1

...

Transaction Summary
================================================================================
Install      34 Package(s)
Upgrade     214 Package(s)
Remove        2 Package(s)

Total download size: 253 M
Downloading Packages:
(1/248): acl-2.2.49-6.9.amzn1.x86_64.rpm                     |  83 kB     00:00
(2/248): alsa-lib-1.0.22-3.9.amzn1.x86_64.rpm                | 434 kB     00:00
(3/248): alsa-lib-devel-1.0.22-3.9.amzn1.x86_64.rpm          | 1.4 MB     00:00
(4/248): apr-util-1.3.9-3.11.amzn1.x86_64.rpm                |  95 kB     00:00

...

(247/248): zlib-1.2.3-27.9.amzn1.x86_64.rpm                  |  78 kB     00:00
(248/248): zlib-devel-1.2.3-27.9.amzn1.x86_64.rpm            |  45 kB     00:00
--------------------------------------------------------------------------------
Total                                        7.5 MB/s | 253 MB     00:33
Running rpm_check_debug
Running Transaction Test
Transaction Test Succeeded
Running Transaction
Warning: RPMDB altered outside of yum.
  Updating   : libgcc-4.4.6-3.45.amzn1.x86_64                             1/473
  Updating   : setup-2.8.14-13.9.amzn1.noarch                            2/473
  Installing : perl-Encode-Locale-1.02-3.1.amzn1.noarch                  6/473

...

  zlib.i686 0:1.2.3-27.9.amzn1
  zlib.x86_64 0:1.2.3-27.9.amzn1
  zlib-devel.x86_64 0:1.2.3-27.9.amzn1

Replaced:
```

```
jpackage-utils.noarch 0:1.7.5-3.12.13.amzn1
mysql.x86_64 0:5.1.61-1.27.amzn1
mysql-devel.x86_64 0:5.1.61-1.27.amzn1
mysql-libs.x86_64 0:5.1.61-1.27.amzn1
```

Complete!

I know this listing is a bit long, but pay close attention to the parts that are **bold**. These are the key milestones in the update process.

1. Yum examines all the software on the instance and sees what needs to be updated.
2. It then checks to see what dependencies those packages have, and continues to do so recursively until it has an exhaustive list of all the software packages that need to be downloaded.
3. Yum downloads all the required packages.
4. Yum installs the updates, cleans up, and indicates the process is complete.

You should never see an error with this script. On the off chance that you do, find yourself a qualified Linux administrator to troubleshoot it for you. To be frank, though, there's nothing terribly out of the ordinary about your server, and Amazon does an exceptional job of making sure that updates will work on their stock instances before releasing them into the wild.

PBX Module Updates

The various software modules in FreePBX need to be updated from time to time as well. You can do this through the Web interface by clicking Admin → Module Admin → Check Online → Upgrade All → Process → Apply.

Figure 7-6. Module updates step 1

Figure 7-7. Module updates step 2

The other way to do it, however, is to add it to the daily update script that you just created. To do so, just execute the following commands:

```
sudo -i
cd /tmp/cron.daily
echo "/var/lib/asterisk/bin/module_admin upgradeall" >> upgrade.sh;
echo "/var/lib/asterisk/bin/module_admin reload" >> upgrade.sh;
echo "amportal restart" >> upgrade.sh;
```

These commands are adding three new directives to the upgrade.sh script you created earlier.

The first command appends to the script the directive to go out and update all the eligible FreePBX modules. The second directive reloads the FreePBX core engine with the upgrades. The final directive restarts the Asterisk PBX software.

You can test this script—as before—by simply typing:

```
./upgrage.sh
```

Recovering from Disaster

Nobody thinks that a disaster is going to strike one of their machines, but someday it will happen. It always does.

Thanks to your nightly snapshots, you will be able to recover very quickly.

Restoring an Instance to a Previous Snapshot

Sometimes it's necessary to restore an instance to a previous state. The easiest way to do this is via one of your nightly snapshots.

This process is pretty straightforward, but there are one or two "gotchas" to watch out for.

1. From the EC2 instance management page, right-click the instance and stop it.
2. Click the Snapshots link on the left.
3. Right-click the snapshot you want to restore from and select Create Volume from Snapshot.
4. Give the new volume a meaningful name and description.

Gotcha #1: When creating a new volume from an existing snapshot, make certain you specify a volume size *at least* as large as the size of the snapshot. You can make the volume bigger, if you like, but you should never try to shrink it.

5. Click the Volumes link on the left and hit the Refresh button in the upper right until you see that your volumes are 100 percent created.

6. Right-click the volume *currently* being used by your instance and select Detach Volume. This might take a minute or two depending on the volume size.

7. Right-click the volume you *just* created and select Attach Volume.

8. In the window that pops up, select the instance that you want to restore.

9. In the Device field, type **/dev/sda1**.

 Gotcha #2: I don't care what the pop-up window suggests you call your device: you must *always* make it **/dev/sda1**. The reason is that all the AMIs you've been using expect their boot volumes to be attached as that device. If you attach your volume as a different device, your instance will not boot.

10. Select Yes—Attach.

You can now safely right-click your instance and start it. You will find after it starts that it is in the condition it was at the moment your snapshot was taken.

 Don't forget to delete the volume that is no longer attached to your instance!

Creating a New Instance from a Snapshot

Sometimes you will want to create a brand-new instance from a snapshot you have already taken. This process is very similar to the one I just described but has a couple of key extra steps in the beginning.

1. Right-click the instance you want to copy and select Launch More Like This.

2. Go through the wizard and be sure to give your new instance a meaningful name.

3. When you complete the wizard, the new instance will begin to start. Right-click it and stop it.

4. Now simply follow the steps from the previous section to set up your new instance from the snapshot of your choice.

The same caveat applies as earlier about deleting the newly detached volume.

Wrapping Up

Fretting over the health of your network isn't necessarily the most exciting thing you can do with your time, but it's a vital aspect of your role as an IT administrator. Each of the topics I've covered in this chapter could easily be a chapter unto itself, so I encourage you to supplement your reading with the documentation from Amazon and perhaps a good Linux primer.

If you're not especially interested in some of the more esoteric aspects and capabilities of your new infrastructure, you can stop reading here. The final chapter in this book will cover some (I think) fun topics related to how I built some of the AMIs you are using and some really neat things you can use them for. That said, you'll need to be more of a bit-twiddler than I have expected of you thus far to really get the most out of what comes next.

If you feel up to it, then onward we go!

## CHAPTER 8

For Those About to Grok, We Salute You

No matter what subject I'm writing about, I always like to include a chapter or two for the bit-twiddlers in the crowd.

You know who you are.

You're the ones who want to know the innards of how something was done. Just setting up a system isn't good enough for you. You need to know *exactly* how the sausage was made.

This chapter is for you.

In this chapter I'm going to cover the super nitty-gritty of two subjects that I touched on earlier: exactly how to build and compile Asterisk/FreePBX on a stock Amazon AMI, and some of the more valuable uses of SSH in your daily lives.

If you're not really all that interested in the guts of shell scripts or Make files, then you should probably stop reading this book here. On the other hand, if you're like me and *need* to know these things, then you've come to the right place!

Building a PBX from Scratch on a Stock Amazon AMI

What you are about to read is the product of several weeks of research, experimentation, and refinement. To the best of my knowledge it represents the only place in print —or online—where you will get step-by-step instruction on how to take a stock AWS AMI and build a PBX from source code.

At the end of the day, I wound up writing a Bash shell script to automate the process as much as is reasonable. In the next few pages I'm going to take you through that script, section by section, and explain what everything does.

 You don't have to retype all this into your own script! I've put the script on GitHub (*https://github.com/drensin/AWS-Book/blob/master/installAs terisk.sh*).

This first section does three important things:

1. It sets up the script to echo out an error message every time a command in the script returns an error. In addition, it will pause the script until you press a key to continue.

2. The set -x command turns on debugging in the script so you can see every line as it executes.

3. Finally, I create a variable named PASSWORD that will keep the global password for the various things that need to be set up.

 If you're going to run this script to compile your own PBX from scratch, you *must* change the PASSWORD script variable.

```
#! /bin/bash

trap "echo \"##### Script error! ####\"; read" ERR
set -x

export PASSWORD="passw0rd!"
```

It's pretty much a certainty that your AMI will be slightly out of date the moment you launch it, so the first thing to do is to update everything. The -y option tells yum not to prompt you for permission or progress.

```
yum -y update
```

The prebuilt modules you need to install in your AMI are stored in repositories. Amazon maintains a special set of those repositories specifically for its stock Linux images. Unfortunately, not all the software you will need for this build is contained in the default Amazon repositories. It will be necessary for you to register an additional repository for yum to check as you install software.

Not all repositories are created equal, however, and you want to be very careful which ones you install software from. Some years ago, Red Hat established the EPEL repository. EPEL stands for Extra Packages for Enterprise Linux and is pretty much the gold standard for third-party package repositories.

The following command in the script registers the latest EPEL repository with the Yum package manager on the running instance.

```
rpm -Uvh http://download.fedoraproject.org/pub/epel/6/i386/epel-
release-6-7.noarch.rpm
```

With the EPEL configured, the script will then install certain key groups of packages. These include a standard development tool chain for compiling, a Web server, and a database.

These components are required because FreePBX runs on what's known as the *LAMP* stack. LAMP stands for Linux, Apache, MySQL, and PHP. These technologies are so often used together that people just refer to them generically by their acronym.

Installing the following package groups is the first step in getting a LAMP stack running on your AMI.

```
yum -y groupinstall "Development Tools"
yum -y groupinstall "DNS Name Server"
yum -y groupinstall "Web Server"
yum -y groupinstall "Mail Server"
yum -y groupinstall "MySQL Database"
```

These next lines install needed packages that aren't automatically picked up in the previous package groups. They include some familiar faces like the runtime library and development headers for SRTP (libsrtp and libsrtp-devel, which I request together in the script through the shorthand `libsrtp*`) as well as packages like fail2ban and the MySQL development libraries.

```
yum install -y e2fsprogs-devel keyutils-libs-devel krb5-devel libogg libselinux-devel
libsepol-devel libxml2-devel libtiff-devel
yum install -y php gmp php-pear php-pear-DB php-gd php-mysql php-pdo kernel-devel
ncurses-devel audiofile-devel libogg-devel
yum install -y openssl-devel mysql-devel zlib-devel perl-DateManip sendmail-cf sox
yum install -y libsrtp* flite fail2ban php-posix incron mISDN* php-x*
```

The `incron` package is required by the FreePBX System Admin module and is installed on the last line in the previous script block.

```
chkconfig incrond on  Set the incron daemon (incrond) to run automatically
service incrond start  Start the incron service
```

 A daemon (pronounced *DAY-MON*, not *DEE-MON*), is like a Windows service: a software program designed to run unattended.

For all intents and purposes, the next few lines neuter the built-in Linux firewall. This is OK because you have Amazon security groups to protect your AMIs.

```
echo ?SELINUX=disabled? > /etc/selinux/config
```
Disable Security Enhanced Linux (SELINUX) features in the kernel.
```
iptables -P INPUT ACCEPT
```
Set the default behavior of the iptables INPUT queue to accept all connections.
```
iptables -P OUTPUT ACCEPT
```
Set the default behavior of the iptables OUPUT queue to accept all connections.
```
iptables -P FORWARD ACCEPT
```
Set the default behavior of the iptables FORWARD queue to accept all connections.
```
iptables -F
```
Delete all the individual firewall rules.
```
iptables -X
```
Delete any user-defined rule chains.

```
/etc/init.d/iptables save
```
Save the new firewall configuration.

Asterisk needs a library called *LAME* in order to run correctly. LAME is an audio processing library that—among other things—helps programs decode a wide variety of audio formats. As popular as it is, however, LAME is not in either the Amazon or EPEL repositories, so the script has to download the source code and compile/install it.

A couple of important points need to be made here.

First, I'm using a command-line tool named `wget` to download the LAME source code compressed file. The options I'm using tell `wget`:

- Not to overwrite a matching copy of the file if it already exists on disk.
- To try downloading repeatedly in case of failure.
- Not to accept a refused connection as a reason to quit. Servers can get overloaded sometimes and refuse new connections, and I wanted `wget` to keep trying until it got through.

Also note that I always include a command after each `wget` in the script that prompts you to press a key after you are sure the download is complete. Theoretically you shouldn't need this, but on a couple of occasions `wget` decided to launch in the background and I found that the script proceeded as if the download were complete. That was obviously no good, so I built in this safeguard.

I next uncompress the source code package using `tar`, change directories into the newly created subdirectory with the source code, run the standard `configure` script, and compile and install the library via `make`.

A script named `configure` is used almost universally when building a program from source code. Its job is to interrogate the system at a very granular level to make sure that certain prerequisites for the software are met. An example of this is when `configure` checks to see whether certain development headers are present.

A Much Deserved Tip of the Hat

As an aside, the author of the class of tools to which `configure` belongs—GNU Auto Configure (or `autoconf`)—was a really good friend of mine in college named David J. Mackenzie. (He still is a good friend, actually.) He's one of the nicest people you could ever hope to meet, and he taught me more about computer programming while we worked together than every book I own put together. He's probably the smartest computer programmer I've ever known, and I owe a fair amount of my professional success to the skills he so patiently taught me.

Stop by and say hi to him on Facebook (*https://www.facebook.com/dmacnet*) if you like this chapter—he's a big reason I'm able to write it.

```
cd /usr/src
wget -nc -t 0 --retry-connrefused http://downloads.sourceforge.net/project/lame/lame/
3.98.4/lame-3.98.4.tar.gz?ts=1292626574&use_mirror=cdnetworks-us-1

echo "### Wait for download to complete and press a key ###"
read

tar zxvf lame-3.98.4.tar.gz
cd lame-3.98*

./configure

make
make install
```

With LAME successfully out of the way, it's time to download the most current version of the Asterisk source code. Once again, it's wget to the rescue.

```
cd /usr/src
wget -nc -t 0 --retry-connrefused http://downloads.asterisk.org/pub/telephony/
asterisk/asterisk-1.8-current.tar.gz

echo "### Wait for download to complete and press a key ###"
read
```

Now I uncompress the source and run an accompanying script file, which fetches some needed source code for MP3 support from the Web. The Asterisk team doesn't ship this code with the rest of the Asterisk code for legal reasons related to the restrictions on the MP3 format, but you can download the MP3 source separately. (Before you ask, no, I have no idea about the legal particulars.)

Then, it's time for our old friend configure to do its job and make sure that the Asterisk source can be successfully compiled on this AMI.

```
tar zxvf asterisk-1.8*.tar.gz

cd asterisk-1.8*

contrib/scripts/get_mp3_source.sh

./configure
```

Before the code can be compiled, however, some additional configuration needs to be done. Instead of running make on the whole source tree (as I would normally do), I have to build a special configuration menu using the command make menuconfig.

 Before you issue make menuconfig you must make sure your terminal window is at least 80x27 (characters) in size. Most probably the window you're using is only 80x24, since that's what everyone standardizes to. Just use your mouse to make your window a bit taller. If you don't do this, you will get a nasty rebuke from make.

```
echo
echo "## Make sure your terminal window is at least 80x27 ###"
echo "# add-ons - format_mp3, res_config_mysql ###"
echo "# extra sound - EXTRA-SOUND-EN-GSM ###"
echo "# type 's' when done ###"
echo
echo "## press a key when ready ###"
read

make menuconfig
```

When you make menuconfig you will be presented with the following screen.

```
****************************************************
         Asterisk Module and Build Option Selection
****************************************************

                      Press 'h' for help.

          --->  Add-ons (See README-addons.txt)
                Applications
                Bridging Modules
                Call Detail Recording
                Channel Event Logging
                Channel Drivers
                Codec Translators
                Format Interpreters
                Dialplan Functions
                PBX Modules
                Resource Modules
                Test Modules
                Compiler Flags
                Voicemail Build Options
                Utilities
                AGI Samples
                Module Embedding
                Core Sound Packages
                Music On Hold File Packages
                Extras Sound Packages
```

Before you can compile Asterisk to work correctly with FreePBX, you need to go into the Add-ons section and select *format_mp3* and *res_config_mysql*. Then you need to go into the Extra Sound Packages section and select *EXTRA-SOUNDS-EN-GSM*.

When that's done, press s to save the config, and the script continues with the compilation and installation.

The compilation takes several minutes, even on a relatively beefy AMI.

```
make
make install
```

When Asterisk is done compiling and installing, it's time to download and uncompress the FreePBX source code.

```
cd /usr/src
wget -nc -t 0 --retry-connrefused http://mirror.freepbx.org/freepbx-2.10.0.tar.gz

echo "### Wait for download to complete and press a key ###"
read

tar zxvf free*
cd free*
```

This FreePBX installation keeps its main configuration in a MySQL database. Before I can compile and install FreePBX, I need to first prepare these databases.

Step 1 is to make sure that MySQL is running and is configured to always run.

```
service mysqld start
chkconfig mysqld on
```

In order, the next lines do the following:

1. Create a new database named *asterisk*. This is where the main Asterisk/FreePBX settings will be housed.

2. Create a new database named *asteriskcdrdb*. The details of each phone call through the PBX are captured in a Call Detail Record (CDR). This database is where the CDRs are stored.

3. FreePBX ships with a SQL script to create the tables and indexes it needs. This line runs the script for the Asterisk database.

4. The next line does the same for the CDR database.

5. Normally in this installation, you would have to go into the MySQL console and grant all privileges to the user *asterisk* in both the main and CDR databases. In the next two lines I first create a temporary script file to do this for you and then apply it.

6. Lastly, I change the password for the MySQL root user to the PASSWORD variable set earlier.

```
mysqladmin create asterisk
mysqladmin create asteriskcdrdb
mysql asterisk < SQL/newinstall.sql
mysql asteriskcdrdb < SQL/cdr_mysql_table.sql

echo "GRANT ALL PRIVILEGES ON asteriskcdrdb.* to asteriskuser@localhost IDENTIFIED BY
'$PASSWORD'; GRANT ALL PRIVILEGES ON asterisk.* to asteriskuser@localhost IDENTIFIED
BY '$PASSWORD'; flush privileges; \q" > testsql.sql

mysql < testsql.sql

mysqladmin -u root password $PASSWORD
```

I just told MySQL that the system user named *asterisk* has special permissions to the databases. The problem is that I haven't created that user on the system yet!

First, I add the user and assign it a home directory of */var/lib/asterisk*. Then I change ownership of certain key directories to be controlled by the `asterisk` user or anyone in the `asterisk` group.

```
useradd -c "Asterisk PBX" -d /var/lib/asterisk asterisk

chown -R asterisk:asterisk /var/run/asterisk
chown -R asterisk:asterisk /var/log/asterisk
chown -R asterisk:asterisk /var/lib/php/session/
chown -R asterisk:asterisk /var/lib/asterisk
```

I particularly like this next bit in the script.

Normally I would have to hand edit the Apache configuration file (*/etc/httpd/conf/httpd.conf*) to:

- Change the value of `AllowOverride` from `None` to `All`.
- Change the user that Apache runs as from `apache` to `asterisk`.
- Change the group that Apache runs under from `apache` to `asterisk`.
- Uncomment the `#Servername` line and change the default value from `www.exam ple.com` to the actual machine name of your AMI.

Or … you can automate all this with the following single line of code.

This line takes the default configuration file and performs the four text transformations I just outlined using a wonderful little tool named `sed`.

The result is saved in place (the `-i` option) over the existing file. The line continuation characters (\) at the end of the lines are just for readability. This is all one line of code to the shell interpreter.

```
sed -i -e "s/AllowOverride None/AllowOverride All/g" \
       -e "s/User apache/User asterisk/g" \
       -e "s/Group apache/Group asterisk/g" \
       -e "s/\#ServerName www.example.com\:80/ServerName $HOSTNAME\:80/g" \
   /etc/httpd/conf/httpd.conf
```

 If you find yourself regularly at a terminal prompt and aren't familiar with `sed`, you're missing an important tool from your administrative toolbox. You can find the complete documentation for *sed* (*http://uni xhelp.ed.ac.uk/CGI/man-cgi?sed*) and a helpful tutorial (*http://www.gry moire.com/Unix/Sed.html*) online. If you really want to go in-depth, the generally regarded best reference on the subject is the O'Reilly book *sed & awk* (*http://shop.oreilly.com/product/9781565922259.do*).

With the `httpd` changes made, it's time to start both the Web server and the mail server and make sure that they are both configured to always run.

```
service httpd start
service sendmail start
```

```
chkconfig httpd on
chkconfig sendmail on
```

For FreePBX to install correctly, the core Asterisk application must be running in a certain way. The `./start_asterisk` script found in the FreePBX source tree will start it in just the correct fashion.

```
./start_asterisk start
```

By default, PHP is not configured for any particular time zone. FreePBX hates that, so the following line configures it for EST by setting it to New York City. In general you should set this value to match the AWS availability zone in which your AMI is running. Mine is in `us-east-1a` (the east coast of the United States), which is why I used this value.

```
echo "date.timezone = America/New_York" >> /etc/php.ini
```

Now that the preliminaries are out of the way, it's time to install FreePBX. This is done via the `install_amp` script in the FreePBX source tree. By default, it will try to use the default `asterisk` username and password, but we've just changed those, so I add the `--username` and `--password` options to tell it explicitly under what account to log in.

```
./install_amp --username=asteriskuser --password=$PASSWORD
```

Go ahead and accept all the default options that `install_amp` gives you until you come to this question:

```
Enter the IP ADDRESS or hostname used to access the AMP web-admin:
[192.168.1.1]
```

For this value, enter **localhost** or **127.0.0.1**. Either will be fine.

When `install_amp` finishes I add a new command—`amportal`—to run at bootup from the */etc/rc.local* file. `amportal start` will gracefully start Asterisk.

```
echo "/usr/local/sbin/amportal start" >> /etc/rc.local
```

Almost done!

Some of the FreePBX modules I want to install have their source code protected by a product named Zend Guard. In order to use those modules, PHP has to be configured to load the Zend Guard Loader helper library when it runs, or it won't be able to interpret the protected code.

These next lines download, uncompress, and copy the ZendGuardLoader library to a place PHP can find it.

```
wget -nc -t 0 --retry-connrefused http://downloads.zend.com/guard/5.5.0/
ZendGuardLoader-php-5.3-linux-glibc23-x86_64.tar.gz

echo "### Wait for download to complete and press a key ###"
read

tar -zxvf ZendGuardLoader*
```

```
mkdir /usr/local/lib/php/

cp ZendGuardLoader*/php-5.3.x/ZendGuardLoader.so /usr/local/lib/php/
ZendGuardLoader.so
```

Next, I add two lines to the end of the PHP configuration file to tell it to use the new library and where it is located.

After that, the Web server has to be restarted.

In order to make sure that PHP is now set up correctly, I issue the command `php -v`, which prints the version information for PHP. I also pause the script so you can validate the output.

```
echo "zend_optimizer.optimization_level=15" >> /etc/php.ini
echo "zend_extension=/usr/local/lib/php/ZendGuardLoader.so" >> /etc/php.ini

service httpd restart
php -v

echo "## check php ##"
read
```

The result of `php -v` should look like the following. The part in **bold** is the part that tells you that the Zend Guard Loader is correctly installed and ready.

```
PHP 5.3.14 (cli) (built: Jul  3 2012 00:28:02)
Copyright (c) 1997-2012 The PHP Group
Zend Engine v2.3.0, Copyright (c) 1998-2012 Zend Technologies
    with Zend Guard Loader v3.3, Copyright (c) 1998-2010, by Zend Technologies
```

In a normal FreePBX installation, you would have to go to the administrative Web page and install and update the core modules.

No such hassle here!

Enables the default FreePBX 2.10 UI framework. Why that's not done automatically in the installation is beyond me, but it isn't.
```
/var/lib/asterisk/bin/module_admin enable framework
```

Enables the supplemental ARI framework.
```
/var/lib/asterisk/bin/module_admin enable fw_ari
```

Installs all the FreePBX modules that ship with the source code but aren't automatically enabled or installed.
```
/var/lib/asterisk/bin/module_admin installall
```

Upgrades all the installed modules.
```
/var/lib/asterisk/bin/module_admin upgradeall
```

Reloads the FreePBX manager to recognize the changes.
```
/var/lib/asterisk/bin/module_admin reload
```

Several commercial modules depend on the System Admin module, which is not installed by default. These next two lines tell the FreePBX module admin tool to locate the System Admin module in any of the FreePBX repositories, download it, install it, and reload the module manager.

```
/var/lib/asterisk/bin/module_admin --repos standard,unsupported,extended,commercial
download sysadmin
/var/lib/asterisk/bin/module_admin --repos standard,unsupported,extended,commercial
install sysadmin
/var/lib/asterisk/bin/module_admin enable sysadmin
/var/lib/asterisk/bin/module_admin reload
```

The next couple of lines look complicated but aren't.

First, I set two variables. I will use the first one to execute a command and the second to insert the same command into the output stream generated by sed.

The process works like this:

1. $CMDSTUB listonline expands to:

   ```
   /var/lib/asterisk/bin/module_admin --repos
   standard,unsupported,commercial,extended listonline
   ```

   which fetches the complete list of all available modules from the four major repositories.

2. sed -E -e "1,4 d" invokes sed. The first expression translates to *lines 1 through 4 delete*. I delete the first four lines of the list because they contain headers I don't want.

3. -e "s/([^]+).+/echo\necho \"#### \1 ####\"\n$CMDSTUB_SAFE install \1\n \n/" just finds the first group of non–white-space characters and inserts them into a command stream that:

   a. Prints a blank line.

   b. Prints the name of the matched text.

   c. Installs the matched text (which will be the name of a module found online) into FreePBX.

4. > getmods.sh just writes the ouput of sed to a new file named *getmods.sh*.

```
export CMDSTUB="/var/lib/asterisk/bin/module_admin --repos
standard,unsupported,commercial,extended"
export CMDSTUB_SAFE="\/var\/lib\/asterisk\/bin\/module_admin --repos
standard,unsupported,commercial,extended"

$CMDSTUB listonline | sed -E -e "1,4 d" -e "s/([^ ]+).+/echo\necho \"#### \1 ####\"\n
$CMDSTUB_SAFE install \1\n\n/" > getmods.sh
```

The first few lines of *getmods.sh* will look similar to the following:

```
echo
echo "#### asterisk-cli ####"
/var/lib/asterisk/bin/module_admin --repos standard,unsupported,commercial,extended
install asterisk-cli
```

```
echo
echo "#### asteriskinfo ####"
/var/lib/asterisk/bin/module_admin --repos standard,unsupported,commercial,extended
install asteriskinfo
```

I next make the new file executable, run it twice, and then clean up by removing it.

The reason I run the script twice is because some modules depend on others and won't necessarily install in the correct order.

For example, module *A* may need module *B* to be installed first. The first time the script runs the installation of module *A*, it will fail because module *B* isn't already installed. The second time it runs, however, it has already installed *B* and the installation of *A* will succeed.

I run the script only twice because there are no sets of module dependencies that go more than one level deep. If there were a case where *A* depended on *B*, which depended on *C*, I would have to run the script three times—the first pass would catch *C*, the next pass would take care of *B*, and the final pass would grab *A*.

```
chmod +x getmods.sh

./getmods.sh
./getmods.sh

rm -f ./getmods.sh
```

Once all the modules are installed and enabled, I restart the module manager and restart Asterisk.

```
/var/lib/asterisk/bin/module_admin reload
```

```
/usr/local/sbin/amportal restart
```

The last step in the basic installation is to enable the fail2ban service and restart the Web server.

```
service fail2ban start
service httpd restart
```

This final section of the script sets up Asterisk to handle encrypted calls via TLS and SRTP.

To do this, a server certificate has to be generated and put someplace Asterisk can find it.

Create a new home for the keys.
```
mkdir /etc/asterisk/keys
```

Go into the Asterisk source tree to the place where the TLS scripts are kept.
```
cd /usr/src/asterisk*/contrib/scripts
```

Run the `ast_tls` *script to generate the server keys in the directory created in step 1.*
```
./ast_tls_cert -C pbx.mycompany.com -O "My Super Company" -d /etc/asterisk/keys
```

Let users other than root be able to read the key files.
```
chmod +r /etc/asterisk/keys/*
```

 Be sure to change the items in bold to:

- The public-facing DNS name of your server
- A description that accurately reflects your company

Asterisk uses dozens of configuration files. Some of them are routinely modified by FreePBX and therefore are not safe places to make configuration changes. Others exist specifically as a safe haven for custom settings.

The safe place to put general SIP configuration customizations is the */etc/asterisk/ sip_general_custom.conf* file.

In this case I add six configuration lines that:

1. Enable TLS support
2. Tell Asterisk to accept TLS connections on any of its network interfaces
3. Set the path to the server certificate file generated in the previous code section
4. Set the path to the CA certificate file, since these are self-signed certificates
5. Permit Asterisk to negotiate and accept any valid TLS encryption method
6. Tell Asterisk to talk to TLS clients using the least common denominator: TLS Version 1.0

I then restart Asterisk again to grab the changes, and the script ends.

```
echo "tlsenable=yes" >> /etc/asterisk/sip_general_custom.conf
echo "tlsbindaddr=0.0.0.0" >> /etc/asterisk/sip_general_custom.conf
echo "tlscertfile=/etc/asterisk/keys/asterisk.pem" >> /etc/asterisk/
sip_general_custom.conf
echo "tlscafile=/etc/asterisk/keys/ca.crt" >> /etc/asterisk/sip_general_custom.conf
echo "tlscipher=ALL" >> /etc/asterisk/sip_general_custom.conf
echo "tlsclientmethod=tlsv1" >> /etc/asterisk/sip_general_custom.conf

/usr/local/sbin/amportal restart

echo "### DONE! ####"
```

 Just because you've compiled Asterisk and FreePBX from scratch does not make them secure. For one thing, the default admin password is *admin*! Go back to Chapter 6 and be certain to go through all the security and configuration steps I outlined there. If you don't, you have just spent a bunch of time giving some hacker free access to your PBX.

Inside SSH—The Really Useful Edition

A shocking number of administrators I know who interact with Linux—or some other Unix-style variant—every day have never even heard of sed, much less used it. To me, not knowing the names of all the tools in your toolbox is one of two serious sins a good system admin can commit.

The greater sin—in my opinion—is underestimating the values of the tools you *do* know about.

SSH is perhaps the best example of a tool every admin uses but few truly appreciate. In this section I'm going to cover some of my favorite SSH tricks that I think you will need as you administer your new network.

Teleportation

At one time or another all of us have dreamed of being able to snap our fingers and be instantly someplace else. The combination of SSH and AWS let you do that, in a way.

Let me explain...

The Amazon cloud exists in eight geographic regions around the world. They are:

- US East (Northern Virginia)
- US West (Oregon)
- US West (Northern California)
- EU (Ireland)
- Asia Pacific (Singapore)
- Asia Pacific (Tokyo)
- South America (Sao Paulo)
- AWS GovCloud (*http://aws.amazon.com/govcloud-us/*)—reserved solely for the use of government customers

Suppose you live in Northern Virginia (as I do) but stand up an instance in Oregon. Processes that run from that Oregon instance will look to the outside world like they're originating from the west coast of the United States—because they are.

Suppose further that—for the sake of my personal privacy—I wanted to prevent the websites I visited from knowing my true IP address or where I lived. There are pay services that will help you with this, and a few open source projects dedicated to the problem, but you don't need any of them. You already have all the tools you need.

If you're reading this chapter, you already know what a Web proxy server is. You might even know that the most recent class of proxy servers uses a protocol called SOCKS (*http://en.wikipedia.org/wiki/SOCKS_(protocol)*).

I'll wager you didn't know that SSH has a SOCKS proxy built right into it! That means I can securely connect from my home in Virginia to my server in Oregon via SSH and use the built-in SOCKS proxy to make all my Web traffic (and lots of other kinds of traffic, too) look like it's originating from the west coast.

To do this is a two-step process.

Step 1 is to connect from my client computer to my server via SSH with the -D command-line option. Normally I would connect to an Amazon instance in the following way:

```
ssh -i dkr-ec2.pem ec2-user@my_instance_ip_address
```

To use SOCKS, I add an additional command-line argument as follows:

```
ssh -i dkr-ec2.pem -D 1080 ec2-user@my_instance_ip_address
```

This additional argument sets up the built-in SOCKS proxy to listen to the local port 1080.

Step 2 is achieved by telling my browser of choice to use a SOCKS proxy, specifying that the proxy is at:

- Host: localhost
- Port: 1080

If you're a Windows user, you can achieve the same outcome via the GUI in PuTTY.

Of course, privacy isn't the only reason I might want the rest of the world to think I'm someplace else.

As a part of my job I travel overseas quite a bit. Some of my favorite Web services (I'm looking at *you*, Hulu!) are restricted to the United States only. I pay Hulu every month for their Hulu+ service, and I don't think it's fair that I be denied something I paid for just because I happen to be traveling.

Using the proxy trick I can (and do) easily make Hulu think I'm still in the States even when I'm in some unpleasant place ending in -stan or -geria.

Moral judgments aside, that's a pretty handy trick!

SSH as a Poor Man's VPN

An even lesser-known feature of SSH is that it can securely forward *any* port (or set of ports). This is ridiculously handy.

Suppose I have a Linux AMI running in a VPC; the AMI has a public DNS name of *pbx.dkrdomain.com*, and it has SSH enabled for its security group.

Further suppose that I have another machine in my VPC with a local VPC address of 10.0.0.14, and that this instance is running a Web server that I don't want exposed to the rest of the world.

I can:

- Use my VPN to connect to the VPC and then access the Web server
- Use a simple SSH trick to remove the need for the VPN altogether

The first option you already know about. The second is accomplished in the following way:

```
ssh -i dkr-ec2.pem -L 8000:10.0.0.14:80 ec2-user@pbx.dkrdomain.com
```

The -L option lets you redirect a local port via a remote host to a third machine. In this case I'm telling SSH that when I try to connect to my local machine on port 8000, I really want to travel through my secure tunnel to *pbx.dkrdomain.com* and connect to my VPC instance at address 10.0.0.14 on port 80.

This means that the URL *http://localhost:8000* will really be redirected securely through my PBX to the internal instance at 10.0.0.14 on the regular HTTP port of 80. I can now get to my previously inaccessible Web server simply by connecting to my local machine on port 8000.

At this point you might be thinking that this technique is the same as the SOCKS technique. That's only because my example happened to involve Web traffic. Suppose I wanted to RDP to the same machine but didn't want to allow RDP traffic through the firewall.

No problem!

RDP runs on port 3389, so I would change my **ssh** command to:

```
ssh -i dkr-ec2.pem -L 8000:10.0.0.14:3389 ec2-user@pbx.dkrdomain.com
```

Now when I tell my RDP client to connect to my local machine at port 8000, it will really get me to my VPC-internal machine at the heretofore unreachable 10.0.0.14 address.

SSH will even let me string these techniques together in one line, like so:

```
ssh -i dkr-ec2.pem -L 8000:10.0.0.14:80 -L 9000:10.0.0.14:3389 -D 1080
ec2-user@pbx.dkrdomain.com
```

In this case I connect to the remote Web server from the local port 8000, RDP to the remote machine from local port 9000, and proxy all my Web traffic through a SOCKS server listening on local port 1080.

There are hundreds of useful things SSH can do for you besides just giving you a secure remote shell. Read up on it. You'll be glad you did.

Really, Really Wrapping Up

This is usually the place where I sum up what you've learned and preview the next chapter. As this is the last chapter, only the first of these applies.

Hopefully your inner bit-twiddler had some fun learning how to compile and install your PBX from scratch and exploring some of the neat things SSH can do for you. I know I enjoyed writing about them.

What's next? That's up to you.

You now have a very functional enterprise-grade network running in a world-class cloud. You know how to add services to it and keep it healthy. You even know how to migrate your own VMs to it. From this point on you should be well equipped to handle whatever IT task you may need to take on for your new baby.

I strongly encourage you to read more about all the software that you are now running and to dig deeper into the guts of how these applications work.

It's been my great pleasure bringing this book to life, and I hope you have gotten as much from reading it as I have from writing it.

About the Author

Dave started his career designing and developing software applications and information systems to carry sensitive data over both wired and wireless networks, for clients such as the US Army, the Treasury Department, the Secret Service, and the National Guard Bureau. For his work, Dave received a civilian commendation from the US Army.

In 1997 Dave founded one of the first business divisions in the United States to develop custom applications for the Palm. His success at developing a solution for syncing data between handheld devices and corporate backend systems led to the creation of RiverBed Technologies in 1998. RiverBed's Scout software was eventually licensed to nearly every major manufacturer of handheld devices in the world. In 2000 Dave was named a Mobile Innovator of the Year by *Mobile Computing* magazine.

Get even more for your money.

Join the O'Reilly Community, and register the O'Reilly books you own. It's free, and you'll get:

- $4.99 ebook upgrade offer
- 40% upgrade offer on O'Reilly print books
- Membership discounts on books and events
- Free lifetime updates to ebooks and videos
- Multiple ebook formats, DRM FREE
- Participation in the O'Reilly community
- Newsletters
- Account management
- 100% Satisfaction Guarantee

Signing up is easy:

1. **Go to: oreilly.com/go/register**
2. **Create an O'Reilly login.**
3. **Provide your address.**
4. **Register your books.**

Note: English-language books only

To order books online:
oreilly.com/store

For questions about products or an order:
orders@oreilly.com

To sign up to get topic-specific email announcements and/or news about upcoming books, conferences, special offers, and new technologies:
elists@oreilly.com

For technical questions about book content:
booktech@oreilly.com

To submit new book proposals to our editors:
proposals@oreilly.com

O'Reilly books are available in multiple DRM-free ebook formats. For more information:
oreilly.com/ebooks

O'REILLY®

Spreading the knowledge of innovators   oreilly.com

.

9 781449 333584